W0013722

BOMBA

ORA
PRO NOBIS

Myriam Kaye is a freelance journalist. Three years of residence in India convinced her that Bombay is 'one of the most exciting commercial and cultural capitals in the world.' Her basis of comparison includes postings to cities such as London, Tokyo and Chicago. Asia remains her abiding interest, as reflected in the Asian focus of her academic career (culminating in a master's degree in Art and Art History from Wesleyan University, Connecticut). She has spent 30 years all over Asia, from Hokkaido to Swat, and speaks Chinese, Japanese, Indonesian and Hindustani.

Luca Tettoni, born in northern Italy, is one of the leading Western photographers working in Southeast Asia and the Indian subcontinent. He has travelled extensively in India since the early '70s. His interest in Indian art is expressed in two authoritative volumes on the subject written by Indian scholar C Sivaramamurti. In recent years, Luca Tettoni has contributed to more than 20 titles on Asian art, culture and travel.

BOMBAY & GOA

Myriam Kaye

Photography by Luca Invernizzi Tettoni

ODYSSEY GUIDES
Hong Kong

Grateful acknowledgement is made to the following authors and publishers for permissions granted:

John Murray (Publishers) Ltd. and Harriet Wasserman Literary Agency Inc. for *Heat and Dust* by Ruth Prawer Jhabvala

John Murray (Publishers) Ltd. and Philip & Pamela Joseph Agency for *India File* © Trevor Fishlock 1983

William Morrow & Company Inc. for *India: Labyrinths in the Lotus Land* © Sasthi Brata 1985

Aitken & Stone Ltd for *An Area of Darkness* © V S Naipaul 1964

Anthony Sheil Associates Ltd for *My Days* © R K Narayan 1973/4, first published in the United Kingdom by Chatto & Windus Ltd.

Distribution in the UK, Ireland, Europe and certain Commonwealth countries by Hodder & Stoughton, Mill Road, Dunton Green, Sevenoaks, Kent, TN13 2YA

Series Editors: Bikram Grewal, May Holdsworth, Ralph Kiggell and Toby Sinclair
Map artwork: Bai Yiliang
Design: Janice Lee
Cover Concept: Raquel Jaramillo and Aubrey Tse
Artwork: Au Yeung Chui Kwai
Photography: Luca Invernizzi Tettoni, Photobank; Alain Evrard 9, 18, 43, 66, 81, 89, 92-93

ISBN: 962-217-178-8

British Library Cataloguing in Publication Data has been applied for.

Produced by Twin Age Ltd
Printed in Hong Kong

Cover: Bombay University clock tower

Contents

Maps

Special Topics

Excerpts

Victoria Terminus, Bombay

West India
Indore
Mhow
Tawa Reservoir
Vadodara (Baroda)
Narmada
Warud
Tapti
Surat
Nagpur
Ajanta
Silvassa
Ellora
Dhuldabad
Nasik
Ozar (Ojhar)
Aurangabad
Godavari
Thane
Nanded
Ahmadnagar
Bombay
MAHARASHTRA
Lonavala
Pune (Poona)
Kirkee
Bidar
Solapur (Sholapur)
Shavardhan
Mahabaleshwar
Secunderabad
Satara
Bhima
Gulbarga
Hyderabad
Ratnagiri
Bijapur
Kolhapur
Krishna
ANDHRA
Aihole
Badani
Patadkal
Tungabhadra
Belgaum
PRADESH
Mapusa
Dharwad
KARNATAKA
Kampli
Panaji (Panjim)
Hampi
Margao
Hubli
Tungabhadra Reservoir
Hospet
Guntakal
GOA
Bellary
Karwar
N
Anantapur
Jog Falls
Penukonda
0 50 100 150 km
0 50 100 miles
Lepakshi
To Bangalore
© The Guidebook Company Ltd

Introduction

Old 'India hands', especially the foreign ones, often pronounce that Bombay is, in some way, 'not India'. True, the bustling, upbeat metropolis is in sharp contrast to the inertia of the rest of India. But, in one way, Bombay is the most essential part of the country: it is India's dream of itself.

Superficially, at least, it is a dream of modernity — the skyscrapers, the atomic power plants, the harbour full of up-to-date warships, the neon-lit boulevards, the stores crammed with consumer wares. Given the prevailing lack of quality control, these 20th-century blandishments often prove dream-like, too, in their insubstantiality.

Prosperity is another name for the dream. The five-star glitz, the splashy weddings and sybaritic clubs — this dream, too, has a way of fading before the taxman's chilling glare, for nothing so scandalizes the bureaucrats, intellectuals and political ideologues of the rest of India as Bombay's conspicuous consumption.

Yet this is the facet of the city that retails itself through the cinematic 'dream machine', drawing dispossessed millions from the countryside to Dadar Railway Station and Victoria Terminus in search of a piece of the fabled action.

The dream can turn sour: Bombay's slums and *chawls* (tenements), its drug dens and red-light districts, are as grim as any. Half the population sleeps on the streets. But this socially explosive situation somehow never detonates and Bombay remains one of the safest cities in the world. It is as though even the have-nots see their condition as dream-like and transient, with hope of change.

For the city is forever in flux. Appearances can be as deceptive as a covey of capering *hijras* (eunuchs in drag), or the portentous Victorian façade of public buildings (behind which pure anarchy and bureaucratic inertia prevail), or the unassuming little hillock of Elephanta Island (which hides a classic, millennium-old cave temple).

Incongruities abound: red-tiled Iberian-style villages nestled amidst grimy mills, Brahminic bulls sauntering amidst downtown office blocks, gaudy fishing skiffs drawn up alongside high-rise condominiums, ancient tanks and shrines (complete with ash-smeared fakirs) surrounded by gimcrack skyscrapers, lateen-rigged sailing dhows darting amongst submarines and aircraft carriers.

When the phantasmagoria gets too fervid, Bombay-*wallahs* escape to Goa. The grace and languor of the erstwhile Portuguese colonial enclave amount to a dream-within-a-dream, a respite from the roiling fantasy life of the metropolis. Goa's reverie is as carefree as Bombay's dream is restless.

A Voluntary Suttee

They spoke of the sanctity of religious practices, even took into account the possibility of voluntary suttee: but came to the conclusion that, when all was said and done, it was still suicide and in a particularly gruesome form.

"I know," Olivia said miserably. She had no desire to recommend widow-burning but it was everyone else being so sure—tolerant and smiling but sure*—that made her want to take another stand. "But in theory it is really, isn't it, a* noble *idea. In theory," she pleaded. Without daring to glance in Douglas' direction, she knew him to be sitting very upright with his thin lips held in tight and his eyes cold. She went on rather desperately: "I mean, to want to go with the person you care for most in the world. Not to want to be alive any more if he wasn't."*

"It's savagery," Dr Saunders declared. "Like everything else in this country, plain savagery and barbarism. I've seen some sights in my hospital I wouldn't like to tell you about, not with ladies present I wouldn't. Most gruesome and horrible mutilations—and all, mind you, in the name of religion. If this is religion, then by gad!" he said, so loudly and strongly that the old head-bearer with the hennaed beard trembled from head to foot, "I'd be proud to call myself an atheist."

But Major Minnies—perhaps out of gallantry—rallied to Olivia's side with an anecdote that partly bore out her point of view. It was not something that had happened to him personally but a hundred years earlier and to Colonel Sleeman when in charge of the district of Jabalpore. Sleeman had tried to prevent a widow from committing suttee but had been defeated by her determination to perish together with her husband's corpse.

"That really was a voluntary suttee," Major Minnies told Olivia. "Her sons and the rest of her family joined Colonel Sleeman in attempting to prevent her, but it was no use. She was determined. She sat for four days on a rock in the river and said that if she wasn't allowed to burn herself then she'd starve herself to death. In any case she wasn't going to be left behind. In the end Sleeman had to give way—yes he lost that round but I'll tell you something—he speaks of the old lady with respect. She wasn't a fanatic, she wasn't even very dramatic about it, she just sat there quietly and waited and said no, she wanted to go with her husband. There was something noble there," said the Major—and now he wasn't being tolerant and amused, not in the least.

"Too noble for me, I fear," said Beth Crawford—as hostess, she probably felt it was time to change the tone. "Fond as I am of you, dear man," she told her husband across the table, "I don't really think I could—"

"Oh I could!" cried Olivia, and with such feeling that everyone was silent and looked at her. Douglas also looked—and this time she dared raise her eyes to his: even if he was *angry with her. "I'd want to. I mean, I just wouldn't want to go on living. I'd be* grateful *for such a custom."*

Their eyes met across the table. She saw his hard look melt away into tenderness. And she felt the same way towards him. Her feelings became so strong that she could not go on looking into his eyes. She looked down at her plate, meekly began to cut the hard piece of chicken in floury sauce that had replaced the hard piece of fried fish of the preceding course: and thought that really everything was quite easy to bear and overcome just as long as she and Douglas felt the way they did for each other.

Ruth Prawer Jhabvala, Heat and Dust

But Goa, with its sense of history, still remains rooted in time. The truly timeless facet of western India abides in Ajanta and Ellora. The millennia-old caves there present, in their pure and harmonious form, the full panoply of ancient Deccan iconography and material culture. The anonymous artists even left finely detailed character studies in their portraits and crowd scenes.

Returning to the city, prepare for a shock of recognition at finding some of the same faces peering out of double-decker buses, some of the same icons adorning *paan* stalls or lorries. It is as though Ajanta and Ellora encapsulate the deepest stratum of western India's subconscious, the bedrock of Bombay's dream.

Facts for the Traveller

Visas

All foreign visitors to India require a valid visa. A tourist visa, valid for 90 days from the date of entry, can be obtained from any Indian embassy, high commission or consulate. If you intend to leave India and return within the 90-day period (such as from a trip to Sri Lanka or Pakistan), then it is worth applying for a double- or triple-entry visa. An extension for a further 90 days can be given to a tourist visa by the Foreigners Regional Registration Office in Bombay (Annexe 2, Office of the Commissioner of Police, Dadabhoy Naroji Road, tel. 268111; open 10 am–5 pm). The visa fee varies from nationality to nationality, with British passport holders paying the most — colonial justice perhaps. If a visit extends beyond 90 days, an Income Tax Clearance Certificate is required at the time of departure. This is available from the main tax office in Bombay.

Climate and Clothing

The period between October and February is the most pleasant time to visit **Bombay**, when the city enjoys a balmy season of blue skies and a cool breeze. From March, the temperature gradually rises and the humidity reaches saturation point. It is very hot just before the monsoon rains break in mid-June. The rains last until September. They come as a welcome relief to Bombayites but when the drainage system fails everyone encounters difficulties getting around town. After the initial few days of flooded roads, however, Bombayites take the downpours and regular drenching in their stride. In September, the humidity and temperature begin to fall. Luckily Bombay does not suffer from the incessant power cuts that plague other parts of India, so offices and hotels remain air-conditioned and bearable through the hot months.

Temperatures in Bombay

	Jan	Feb	Mar	Apr	May	Jun	Jul	Aug	Sept	Oct	Nov	Dec
Max °C	31	32	33	33	33	32	30	29	30	32	33	32
Min °C	16	17	20	24	26	26	25	24	24	23	20	18
Max °F	88	90	91	91	91	90	86	84	86	90	91	90
Min °F	61	63	68	75	79	79	77	75	75	73	68	64

BAI MANIBAI
WIDOW OF LATE
SETH CHATRABHUJ JEEVANDAS J.P.
WHO HAS BUILT THIS BAND STAND
AND PRESENTED TO THE
BOMBAY MUNICIPAL CORPORATION
FOR THE USE OF PUBLIC
SAMVANT 1992 A.D. 1936.
વિજયતે શ્રી નવનીત પ્રભુ.
આ બેન્ડ સ્ટેન્ડ બંધાવી આપનાર કપોળ વાણીઆ
સંવત ૧૯૯૨
સને ૧૯૩૬.

Average Rainfall in Bombay

mm	0	1	0	0	20	647	945	660	309	117	7	1
in	0	0	0	0	0.8	25.5	37.2	26	12.2	4.6	0.3	0

The monsoon-time from June to September is for many the best time to visit **Goa**. There are no crowds and most hotels offer discounts. And, of course, the land turns a lush green and people become happier. The winter is more pleasant, but also the most popular. Over the Christmas–New Year period, you tend to be saddled with a very festive crowd. The pre-monsoon summer months of May and June can be unbearably hot inland, but then there are always the beaches to look forward to.

Temperatures in Panaji, Goa

	Jan	Feb	Mar	Apr	May	Jun	Jul	Aug	Sept	Oct	Nov	Dec
Max °C	31	32	32	33	33	31	29	29	29	31	33	33
Min °C	19	20	23	25	27	25	24	24	24	23	22	21
Max °F	88	90	90	91	91	88	84	84	84	88	91	91
Min °F	66	68	73	77	81	77	75	75	75	73	72	70

Average Rainfall in Panaji

mm	2	0	4	17	18	580	892	341	277	122	20	37
in	0.1	0	0.2	0.7	0.7	22.8	35.1	13.4	10.9	4.8	0.8	1.5

Winter is the busy season at **Ajanta** and **Ellora**. During the summer (April–June), temperatures climb well into the 40s Celsius (over 100 degrees Fahrenheit). The landscape turns parched and dusty. It comes alive again during the monsoon (June–September) and the rain-slicked stone carvings are beautiful, but transportation can be tricky.

Perhaps the best time to visit is at the tail end of the monsoon when the countryside is still a screaming green, temperatures are cooled down and the sculptures, washed by intermittent showers and shifting cloudscapes, produce intriguing variations in the lighting effects. Rainbows, wildflowers and frog and cricket choruses are fringe benefits. By October, it turns hot again for a brief interlude before winter sets in.

Temperatures in Aurangabad (for Ajanta and Ellora)

	Jan	Feb	Mar	Apr	May	Jun	Jul	Aug	Sept	Oct	Nov	Dec
Max °C	29	32	36	38	40	35	29	29	30	31	30	29
Min °C	14	16	20	24	25	23	22	21	21	20	16	14
Max °F	84	90	97	100	104	95	84	84	86	88	86	84
Min °F	57	61	68	75	77	73	72	70	70	68	61	57

Average Rainfall in Aurangabad

mm	3	3	4	7	17	141	189	146	179	62	32	7.6
in	0.1	0.1	0.2	0.3	0.7	5.5	7.4	5.7	7	2.4	1.3	0.3

Clothing Informal, comfortable clothes, preferably in cotton rather than synthetic fibres, will see you through most occasions, but visitors should note that Bombayites are both smarter and more fashion-conscious than the denizens of other Indian cities. Men may want to pack a lightweight jacket and tie for an evening out at a luxury-standard hotel restaurant. Be prepared for chilly air-conditioning and drops in evening temperatures in November–February.

Immunization and Health

India demands yellow fever certificates from travellers arriving from Africa, Latin America and Papua New Guinea. Other shots, although not legally required, are advisable. Typhoid, polio and tetanus are important. A gamma globulin injection against hepatitis A immediately before departure is also recommended. Many countries demand that travellers from India have an up-to-date cholera vaccination. A vaccination against rabies is now available, but you must visit the nearest hospital following any bite from a dog or monkey for a further course of shots.

Malaria is still widespread in many parts of India. Advice as to which pills to take is constantly being revised, but at present Nivaquine (or Avloclor) twice a week and one or two Paludrine daily are suggested. Both courses must be continued for four to six weeks after leaving India.

Most medicines are available in Bombay, but it is always sensible to take a small reserve stock of any prescription drugs. You may also want to put together a basic medical kit in advance of departure; this could usefully include something against 'Delly Belly', antiseptic cream, lip salve, mosquito repellent and soothing cream for bites, suntan lotion for long days on Goa's beaches, water purification tablets if bottled water is not available and elastoplast. Some travellers develop a problem on their second or third day in India because of a lack of acclimatization or heat exhaustion, rather than a reaction to the change in food and water. They are advised to drink lots of fluids (water with a little salt and sugar) and keep to a diet of rice and yoghurt for a couple of days to give their system time to adjust. If an upset stomach persists, seek medical advice (tourist-class hotels have a doctor on call).

There are a few things *not* to do which will make your stay more enjoyable. Never drink tap water (the flasks in hotel rooms contains filtered water and bottled water is now available almost everywhere). Avoid salads, even in hotels, and do not eat the street food until you know how much you can afford to abuse your body for the sake of your palate.

Time Zone

Despite its size, India has a single time zone. It is 2½ hours behind Hong Kong and Singapore, 5½ hours ahead of London (GMT), 4½ hours ahead of British Summer Time, 10½ hours ahead of New York and 13½ hours ahead of San Francisco.

Customs

Visitors are usually asked if they have anything to declare on arrival. An individual should not bring in more than US$1,000 in cash without declaring it. Likewise, video equipment, camera equipment and other high-value items should be declared on arrival. If the customs officer prepares a Tourist Baggage Re-export Form (TBRF) detailing the items declared and their value, then this form must be shown when departing from India. Exchange receipts must also be shown on departure for currency declared.

India allows the standard bottle of spirits, 200 cigarettes and a small

allowance for gift items to be imported free of duty. Indian customs officials are thorough and professional. Usually on the lookout for the smuggler, they rarely trouble the genuine tourist.

On leaving India you may be asked to produce exchange certificates, but this is unlikely unless a declaration was written into your passport on arrival. Traditional souvenirs can be exported without any restriction. Only Rs2,000 worth of gold and up to Rs10,000 worth of ready-made jewellery or precious stones can be exported without a permit. Any object over 100 years old needs an export certificate from the Director of Antiquities, Archaeological Survey of India, Janpath, New Delhi. India is a signatory to CITES and the export of ivory, animal and snake skins, and products made from them, is forbidden. CITES certificates can be issued by the Deputy Director of Wildlife Preservation in Bombay.

Money

As a foreigner, you must pay your air and rail fares and hotel bills with foreign currency, travellers' cheques or international credit cards, unless you can present an encashment certificate to prove you have bought your rupees from an authorized foreign exchange dealer (a bank or a hotel). The amounts of your purchases are noted on the back of your certificate and deducted against the face value. Black market rupee exchange is widely offered at a premium of about 15 per cent.

Photography

The light in India can be harsh, especially during the summer months, so the best time for photography are the 'magic hours' immediately after dawn and before sunset. Photography of airports, railway stations, bridges, military installations and from the air is prohibited. The majority of people do not mind having their photographs taken, but care should be taken in the Muslim quarter of Bombay. If in doubt, ask. Permission is also required to photograph in museums and occasionally to use a flash or tripod inside a monument.

Colour print film is now readily available, but often expensive. Only a limited range of slide film is generally available and no Kodachrome has been imported since the Kodak laboratory in Bombay closed. In short, it is best to bring a good supply of film with you — some people suggest twice what you expect to use. Any film left over at the end of a trip makes a good and welcome present for someone who has been of help.

Things Electrical

Bombay has a good and reliable electricity supply, generated mostly by a private company, Tata Electric, and from the nearby nuclear power station at Thrombay. The voltage is 220 volts, although outside Bombay it tends to fluctuate (usually downwards). Any sensitive equipment, such as a portable computer, should be plugged in through a voltage stabilizer (readily available although bulky). A hotel should be able to lend or arrange the hire of a stabilizer.

Penlight cells and other batteries are available, but not AAA size (except on Bombay's smugglers' market).

Some security checkers at domestic airports not only take away penknives, but also batteries. It is best to put them in your checked baggage.

Communications

Most Bombay hotels have direct dial facilities from the room for both local and international calls. In Goa and Aurangabad it is best to use the hotel operator to connect local and long distance calls. Most hotels have telex facilities and many now have fax lines. Hotels 'mark-up' calls by anything between 100 and 250 per cent, so it is advisable to check each hotel's communications rates before making a lengthy call home. Post varies, but is generally secure and reliable. While a letter only takes three days to arrive from London, it can take up to ten days to get there. Postcards, for some reason, often take longer and parcels take their own time.

Sending registered parcels can be a time-consuming procedure. Most parcels have to be stitched into cheap cotton cloth and then sealed (there are usually people outside major post offices offering this service). Two customs forms also need to be completed. Once the parcel has been weighed and stamps affixed, make sure the stamps are franked and a receipt of registration is given.

Most major international courier companies operate in India offering both domestic and international services.

Beggars

Begging is a fact of life in many countries, but it still comes as a shock to many visitors who encounter it for the first time. In Indian towns, especially around the areas tourists go to, begging is an organized profession. Each gang works an area and the child receiving the alms may not keep more than a small percentage while the leader takes a large cut. If you decide to give to a beggar, a rupee (or less) is enough. Fruit or biscuits are a worthwhile gift to a child beggar, but be discreet — otherwise a crowd will form.

If you want to make a donation, there are numerous worthwhile charities established throughout India. Hotel staff will be able to advise if you wish to give to a reputable charity in the area.

Bombay
First City in India

For millennia before the British came, Bombay was a city waiting to happen. Where the metropolis now stands there were only sleepy villages of Koli fishermen and Bhandari toddy tappers. Key shrines may be thousands of years old, such as the Mumbadevi Temple (from which the city may have derived its name) and the Walkeshwar Tank. But the economic *raison d'être* — the port — dates back only a few centuries.

The magnificent deepwater harbour was too exposed for the naval technology of the ancient world. Instead, the shallow-draught ships of those times gravitated to more sheltered creeks and inlets, so that fabulous ports flourished all around, but never at, the site of present-day Bombay.

Nearby Sopara has been identified as the biblical 'Ophir', purveyor of sandalwood and jewels to ancient Arabia. Kalyan and Thana find mention as great cities in the early Buddhist scriptures. Pliny and Strabo both list major harbours in the area.

All these places are within 56 kilometres (35 miles) of each other, close enough to share a common suburb: the large island of Salsette, which has been inhabited throughout the rise and fall of the neighbouring cities. Ancient cave temples there still survive among the gimcrack modern bedroom townships.

A 'Good Harbour' for the Portuguese

For all their prosperity, though, the Bombay-area seaports had only marginal importance politically. Neither the Hindu kingdoms nor the Muslim sultanates on the subcontinent paid them much attention, leaving them to the charge of minor vassals.

Even the Portuguese, when setting up their string of coastal enclaves in Western India, originally bypassed Bombay in favour of nearby Bassein as their 'northern court'. Only a decade later, almost as an afterthought, did they bother to take the scraggly little archipelago of seven islands that have since been fused together to comprise modern-day Bombay.

Naval forces of the Gujarat sultanate belatedly woke up to the European land-grab and mounted a rearguard defence, inflicting heavy casualties upon the Portuguese. But then, the sultanate, just as abruptly, forgot all about Bombay again. Portugal formally assumed control in 1534 and carved up the territory into fiefdoms to reward its military commanders.

The biggest grants of land went to the monastic religious orders

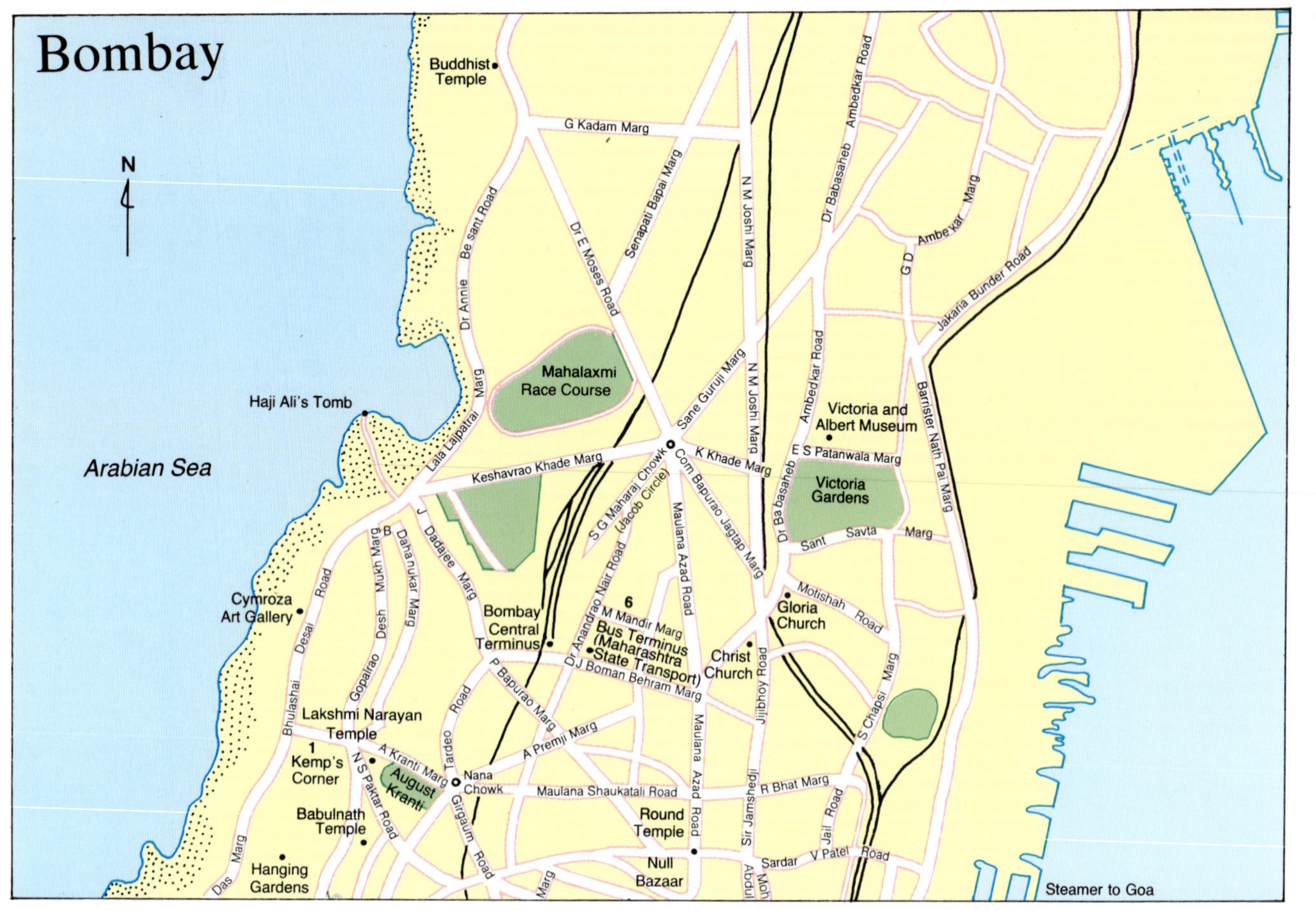
Bombay
N
Arabian Sea
Buddhist Temple
Haji Ali's Tomb
Cymroza Art Gallery
Lakshmi Narayan Temple
1 Kemp's Corner
Babulnath Temple
Hanging Gardens
August Kranti
Nana Chowk
Mahalaxmi Race Course
Bombay Central Terminus
6 Bus Terminus (Maharashtra State Transport)
Christ Church
Gloria Church
Round Temple
Null Bazaar
Victoria and Albert Museum
Victoria Gardens
Steamer to Goa
G Kadam Marg
Senapati Bapai Marg
Dr E Moses Road
Dr Annie Be sant Road
Lala Lajpatrai Marg
Keshavrao Khade Marg
Sane Guruji Marg
N M Joshi Marg
Dr Babasaheb Ambedkar Road
G D Ambekar Marg
Jakaria Bunder Road
Barrister Nath Pai Marg
E S Patanwala Marg
K Khade Marg
Com Bapurao Jagtap Marg
Maulana Azad Road
S G Maharaj Chowk (Jacob Circle)
Dr Anandrao Nair Road
M Mandir Marg
Dr J Boman Behram Marg
Sant Savta Marg
Motishah Road
Jijibhoy Road
S Chapsi Marg
J Dadajee Marg
B Desh Mukh Marg
Dahanukar Marg
Gopalrao Desai Road
Bhulashai Desai Road
Das Marg
N S Paktar Road
A Kranti Marg
Tardeo Road
P Bapurao Marg
A Premji Marg
Girgaum Road
Maulana Shaukatali Road
R Bhat Marg
Sir Jamshedji
Jail Road
Sardar V Patel Road
Abdul Moh
Marg

Kamla Nehru Park
Netaji Subhash Road
Chow patty Beach
Walkeshwar Road
Bal Gangadhar
Laxmibai Jagmohan
Jain Temple
Walkeshwar Temple
Malabar Hill
MALABAR POINT
Back Bay
Aquarium
(Marine Drive)
Netaji Subhash Road
R R M Roy
Jagannath
Maharshi Karve Marg
Dr B Jaykar Marg
Banaji Fire Temple
Mumbadevi Temple
Shankarshet Road
Wadiaji Fire Temple
Kalbadevi Road
Rehman
ammed
Yusuf Ali Road
Meherally Road
Street
Tilak Marg
Nandlal Jani Road
Dr Chormusji Street
Crawford Market
P D'Mello Road
Anjuman Fire Temple
Dr Dadabhai Naoroji Road
Mahapalika Marg
Bombay Victoria Terminus
Azad Maidan
Cross Maidan
Dr V Thackersey Marg
Mahatma Gandhi Road
H Somani Marg
General Post Office
Harbour
CROSS ISLAND
Churchgate
Mint Road
Mehta Road
Mint
Town Hall
Old Customs House
Tourist Office
Flora Fountain
Jamshedji Tata Road
D Wacha Road
Oval Maidan
K B Patil Marg
Horniman (Elphinstone) Circle
Madame Cama Road
Gen J Bhonsle Marg
Band Stand
Cooperage Road
Prince of Wales Museum
C Shivaji Marg
Gateway of India
NARIMAN POINT
Tata Theatre (NCPA)
N Parekh Marg
Singh Road
Bhagat
Sharid
MIDDLE GROUND
World Trade Centre
Capt P Pethe Marg
Sassoon Docks
St John's Church (Afghan Memorial)
1 2 3 4 5 7 8 9 10 11 12
Hotels
1. Shalimar Hotel
2. Fariyas Hotel
3. YWCA/YMCA
4. President Hotel
5. Apollo
6. YMCA
7. Ambassador
8. Astoria
9. Oberoi Towers
10. Taj Mahal Inter Continental
11. Bombay International
12. Ritz
0 0.5 1 1.5 2 km
0 ½ 1 mile
© The Guidebook Company Ltd

which, back in Lisbon, were then at the peak of their political influence. Franciscans and Jesuits, between them, divided the lion's share of Bom Baim (or 'Good Harbour', as the Portuguese had dubbed their new colony). Graft and church-building dominated public life there for the next hundred years.

A Royal Dowry

Small wonder, then, that Bombay never attained the commercial or military importance of other Portuguese colonies. In 1661 Lisbon had few qualms about signing it off (together with Tangier in Africa) as part of the dowry of Princess Catherine of Braganza. She was married to King Charles II of England to cement what turned out to be a short-lived alliance of the two countries against their common rivals, Spain and Holland.

Bombay thus became Britain's first outright Crown colony in India. Previous British toeholds — at Madras, Hooghly near present-day Calcutta, and Surat in Gujarat 240 kilometres (150 miles) north of Bombay — had been in the form of trading concessions, or 'factories', granted by native potentates to the East India Company (EIC).

When it came to actually taking possession of the new colony, though, the reports of the first British expedition sounded a note of distinct disappointment. Far from being a land of fine towns and castles, as it was hyperbolically depicted in earlier British intelligence dispatches, Bombay turned out to be an undeveloped, low-lying, malaria- and cholera-infested swamp. There was also a 'fifth column' of disaffected Portuguese residents to contend with.

Nobody had bothered to consult the local Portuguese in Bombay about the cession of their little enclave. They remained restive for decades after. Jesuits in particular, using their Bandra College as a base, continued to subvert the British administration. The Portuguese falsified land deeds and even the boundaries of the territory. Some early British officials were also only too willing to be suborned.

As a result, government revenues from Bombay dwindled to just one-twelfth of what they had been prior to cession. At the same time, expenses soared as ambitious plans to fortify the main island were implemented. Heading the Bombay administration in the first decade of British rule seemed a luckless task: governors came and went at the rate of one every couple of years.

The first British governor died shortly after prising the territory away from the recalcitrant Portuguese viceroy. The second was condemned for graft, outlawed and banished. The third and fourth incumbents got embroiled in jurisdictional disputes with the Mughal governors and British East India Company's 'presidents' in Surat.

It took barely seven years of such misadventures for the English court to tire of its new colony and fob it off on the EIC to administer. The Company, better informed than the Crown about the actual running costs of an Indian enclave, had already politely declined an offer to run the colony from the outset. But by 1668 Bombay was going at a discount: the Company was happy to take it at an annual rent of ten pounds sterling — a sum that now would not rent space enough for a rope cot in the city's meanest slum.

Enter Aungier

If London undervalued the colony, the EIC's first governor, Gerald Aungier, saw Bombay's potential far more clearly. His memoranda rhapsodized about the impregnability of its island locality (if properly fortified) and the '100-ship' capacity of its monsoon-sheltered harbour. To make the most of these advantages, Aungier realized, a third ingredient was needed: human capital. Economically useful communities had to be attracted to the new colony.

Besides land grants and municipal services, Bombay could offer immigrants an additional blandishment that was unique at that time in Western India — religious toleration. The Portuguese, by contrast, were then in the throes of their Inquisition. As for native Indian rulers, the Mughals, under the zealot emperor Aurangzeb, had provoked an equally fanatical anti-Muslim backlash among the Marathas led by the brilliant guerilla fighter Shivaji.

While the Mughal and Maratha empires battled for control of the countryside, artisans and merchants flocked to Bombay to pursue their business in peace — Muslim weavers from nearby Chaul, Hindu *baniya* bankers and traders, Parsi compradores and shipwrights.

By the time Aungier died in 1677, the Indian population of Bombay had increased sixfold to 60,000. The boom-town growth was too fast for the communities to sift out into segregated ghettos, as in other Indian cities, whether colonial or traditional. Bombay's haphazard intermingling of communities set the city's uniquely cosmopolitan tone from the outset.

Perhaps the least prepossessing ingredient of this melange, at least in the early years of the colony, was the British contingent. Aside from a handful of visionary leaders like Aungier, most of the East India Company's soldiers and functionaries were rapacious, quarrelsome and debauched freebooters. The early annals of British Bombay abound in scandals, duels and brawls.

Things got only worse after the importation of a job lot of English maidens to wean the Company's men away from their 'black velvet' (as the local Koli women were euphemized). The first batch of *memsahibs*

Much of Bombay's money came from cotton cloth manufactured at local mills

(who might not have been recruited from the genteelest of ladies' seminaries back in England) just gave the colonists that much more to quarrel over.

Consolidation
It was not until after the turn of the 18th century that Bombay's civic life became more staid, perhaps in response to a couple of sobering external developments. First, the Company — wary of Maratha pressure on the Mughal enclave of Surat — shifted its Presidency down to Bombay in 1687. Then, barely two years later, the Mughal admiral, Sidi Yakut, with a force of 20,000 men, attacked the city.

Such resistance as Bombay offered was spearheaded by a Koli force under the leadership of a heroic 20-year-old Parsi captain. As for the British, it was nearly 18 months before they bought — rather than fought — their way back in with the payment of a substantial ransom.

With the stake thus raised on the colony, the East India Company stepped up Bombay's development. Land reclamation began in earnest, a Mayor's court was established and — most important of all — the major dockyards were set up. For this task, the Company enticed a Parsi master-shipbuilder from Surat, Lowji Nusserwanji Wadia, to move his operation to Bombay.

This shipyard became a linchpin of British imperial expansion in the Far East. Bombay-built 'China clippers' were the backbone of the lucrative opium trade. The treaty ceding Hong Kong to Britain was signed aboard one of Wadia's ships. The U.S. national anthem was composed aboard another one during a battle in the war of 1812. The Wadias to this day remain a leading Bombay business family.

For all its commercial dynamism, though, early Bombay exerted scant influence over the broader polity of India. In fact, by the mid-18th century, the colony was starting to feel hemmed in by events beyond its control.

Routing Muslim potentates and their French allies in major military victories like Plassey (1759), the British won hinterlands of truly imperial proportions for their enclaves in Calcutta and Madras. No such *Lebensraum* could be claimed for 18th-century Bombay, encircled as it was by the militant Maratha Confederacy headquartered in Poona, just 120 kilometres (75 miles) to the east.

As long as the Peshwas (the confederacy chieftains) held sway, even inland trade remained somewhat circumscribed for Bombay merchants. The city was relegated to the role of an entrepôt and service enclave, not unlike modern Hong Kong. It was not until 1818 that Maratha power was conclusively broken and the Bombay Presidency suddenly found itself heir to a 180,000-square-kilometre (70,000-square-mile) hinterland.

Perhaps thanks to this change in status, the city went on to notch up a series of 'firsts' in the next few decades: first government-backed public educational institutions (Elphinstone High School, 1820, and Elphinstone College, 1819); first large-scale municipal waterworks (1824); first Bombay-built steamship (1829); first through-road over the Ghats (1830, to Poona); first gaslight (1833); first railroad in India (1853, the Bombay–Thana line).

Cotton, Cotton Textiles and Higher Education

The mainspring of all this development was the increasingly important cotton economy. Bombay 'factors' kept the mills of Lancashire supplied with Gujarat cotton. The finished English mill cloth found a major market back in India, shattering local cottage industries in the process — a vicious circle of imperialist exploitation that would eventually rouse revolutionary fervour.

What it roused in the mid-19th century, however, was mainly the venal instinct of Bombay capitalists. If the raw material and the demand for cotton cloth were both in India, why not set up local mills, as well? The first of these started with 17,000 spindles in 1856, immediately attracting a score of imitators.

By that time, Bombay cotton millionaires were already suffering from the classical nouveau riche's yearning for cultural refinement. Hence the establishment in 1857 of the architecturally magnificent Bombay University (see page 83), whose masonry may have outshone its faculty, at least initially. George Bernard Shaw snidely remarked at the time that the height of the University's clocktower might only be exceeded by the depth of its ignorance.

Unfazed by such carping, Bombay went on to establish in the same year an art school, the Sir Jamshedjee Jeejeebhoy School of Art, headed a few years later by Rudyard Kipling's father (whose bas-reliefs still adorn the old Crawford Market pavilions across Mahatma Gandhi Road from the tree-shaded bungalow where Rudyard was born).

With its educational institutions and its concentration of government-related clerical jobs, the city gradually became a magnet for intellectuals and professionals. Later in the century, these groups would provide a fertile field for India's independence movement. But in the 1850s, revolution seemed far from Bombay's collective consciousness.

Even the Great Uprising of 1857, which so traumatized the rest of British India, hardly perturbed the city's upbeat mood. As an object lesson to the garrison, a couple of rabble-rousing sepoys (native troops) were tied to the mouths of cannons and distributed across the

Gandhi in Bombay

Mohandas K Gandhi's visits to Bombay encapsulate his evolution into a Mahatma ('Great Soul'). They also offer vignettes of a city fast transforming itself from an outpost of empire to the cultural and commercial capital of a great and modern nation.

Gandhi first came to the city in 1888 as a shy but determined 17-year-old, en route to England to take up law studies. The Bombay guild of his Gujarati mercantile caste vetoed the trip. Gandhi ignored them and was officially ostracized by his caste. Upon his return, three years later, he tried to practise law in Bombay, but was so overcome by stage fright that he remained tongue-tied in court. Feeling a failure, Gandhi gratefully accepted a face-saving avenue of retreat: an offer from a business group of Gujarati Muslims to argue a contract law case in South Africa.

It was in the anti-discrimination struggle in South Africa that Gandhi first forged his unique blend of personal asceticism and charismatic leadership — a process he detailed in lengthy letters to his spiritual mentor at the time, Raychandbhai, a devout Bombay jeweller.

On his first home visit to India in the course of his 25-year South African interlude, Gandhi sailed into Bombay to find the city in the grip of the great bubonic plague of 1896. He plunged into a public sanitation campaign that led him to visit for the first time the colonies of the outcast 'untouchables' (or Harijans, 'children of God', as Gandhi dubbed them) whose cause he was later to champion.

Although the plague had wiped out a fifth of the population, Bombay soon rebounded and resumed its brisk modernization. Motorcars and electric trams debuted in the city; the premier Parsi business family, the Tatas, opened their glittering waterfront Taj Mahal Hotel; the pompous Gateway of India arch was built to welcome visiting English royalty; a museum was opened. The Lumière brothers called in 1911 to demonstrate their miraculous new invention, sparking Bombay's ongoing love affair with cinematography. A Tata heir took off from Bombay to launch India's first airmail service and airline.

Yet for all this progress, anti-colonial sentiment was gathering momentum. In 1915, the year Gandhi finally returned for good from South Africa, the Congress — at the urging of one of its more promising young luminaries, the dapper, London-educated Muslim barrister, Mohammed Ali Jinnah — scheduled its convention in Bombay to coincide with that of the recently formed Muslim League in a show of solidarity. The British apparently found this combination so threatening that they banned both meetings.

Gandhi, meanwhile, studiously abjured national politics for a year, as prescribed by his political guru, G K Gokhale, the then elder statesman of the independence movement. The object was to re-learn the Indian political landscape.

But Gandhi's perspective was wholly original and compelling — a grass-root view, rather than one focused on the economic and professional elite. The power of his mass mobilization approach soon showed itself in prolonged, non-violent demonstrations and strikes by indigo farmers and Gujarati textile workers, in the course of which Gandhi devised his technique of activist fasting.

Britain chose to reward India's World War I support not with independent Dominion status, as expected by Gandhi and others, but rather with a peacetime extension of the emergency wartime curtailments of civil liberties. In response, Gandhi proclaimed a national non-violent *hartal* (general strike), which he directed largely from Bombay.

The hartal established him as the paramount leader of the fast-accelerating independence drive. The long succession of urbane Anglicized professionals at the helm of the Congress was abruptly interrupted in 1921.

Clad in his characteristic loincloth (which he had only just adopted), Gandhi arrived in Bombay to assume control of an organization that had been restructured to his specifications for grass-roots contact.

A less triumphal arrival was made that same year by the Prince of Wales, who was met with largely deserted streets, in stark contrast to the contrived Gateway of India hoopla at the previous royal visit just nine years earlier. Anti-British riots broke out during the Prince's 1921 stay, and Gandhi had to fast for five days to restore calm.

The Congress, under Gandhi, embarked on a course of 'non-cooperation'. That meant, in principle, cutting off the colonial administration from all Indian revenues, denying British commerce all Indian markets, mass resignation by all Indian civil servants and desertion by all Indian soldiers. Radical as this approach was, most of the Congressmen backed Gandhi, although a few establishmentarians bailed out, including Mohammed Ali Jinnah, the Muslim leader. As for the British, they lost no time in jailing Gandhi.

He spent most of the next decade in and out of jails, fasting intermittently against British inequities, Hindu–Muslim friction and untouchability. In 1930, Gandhi defied the British monopoly on salt production by walking from his Ahmedabad ashram (retreat) to the Surat seashore to collect salt. Although he was courting arrest and police abuse, the mood of his 24-day trek was that of a triumphal march.

By that time, the British viceroy found himself obliged to parley as an equal with 'a half-naked fakir' (as Gandhi was described by a scandalized Winston Churchill). It was to be another 17 years before the formal demise of the Raj, but by 1930, according to Gandhi's biographer, Louis Fischer, the independence battle had already been effectively won.

Whitehall did not quite see it that way, though, and needed some more convincing. By 1942, with the Japanese already entrenched in Burma and menacing India's eastern flank, Gandhi convened the Congress in Bombay to refuse cooperation in the war effort and demand the British 'Quit India' immediately. Massive anti-government demonstrations flared across the country. Churchill, by that time prime minister, was in no mood to entertain ultimatums from the 'fakir', and Gandhi was arrested on the roof of Mandi House near Chowpatty.

By the end of the war the issue was no longer when independence would be granted (since all parties including the British were ready to sever colonial links as quickly as possible), but how to apportion power in the face of rising Hindu–Muslim tensions. Bloody sectarian riots broke out in Bombay and other cities. Jinnah, as head of the Muslim League, spearheaded the drive for a separate 'Land of the Pure' (as the name 'Pakistan' literally translates).

Although himself very much a Bombay sophisticate, married to a Parsi beauty and much given to fine whisky and tailored suits, Jinnah pitched his separatist message at fundamentalist Muslims in the villages and slums. Gandhi danced attendance in Jinnah's Malabar Hill mansion, pleading with him to avert the partition of India.

But the Qaid-e-Azam (Great Leader, as Jinnah was by then styled, both by his followers and by Gandhi) remained unmoved. 'We will have India divided or we will have it destroyed,' he swore.

He almost got it both ways, so violent was the trauma of partition in 1947. Tragically, Gandhi was one of the casualties: he was assassinated by a Hindu zealot who resented his advocacy of Muslim and Harijan interests in the newly independent secular state of India. The Mahatma's last arrival in Bombay was in an urn of cremated ash to be scattered over the Arabian Sea.

Esplanade (nowadays known as Azad Maidan, site of the Gymkhana Club's manicured lawns). This done, the city went about its business.

And business had never been better. The U.S. Civil War, by cutting off Lancashire's cotton supply from America's southern states, created a huge windfall of demand for Gujarat cotton. And just as this boom seemed to be petering out, Bombay's own mill sector emerged strong enough to take up the slack.

The mills required a massive new workforce. A whole new industrial proletariat was imported from the nearby Konkan villages and installed on freshly reclaimed land in the heart of the city.

These Dickensian industrial 'hells', virtually unchanged to this day, provided local business with a practically inexhaustible reservoir of consumer demand. Nowadays, the mill districts also comprise the crucial 'vote banks' of the city's dominant political bosses.

The next serendipitous development in Bombay's favour was the opening of the Suez Canal in 1871, which reduced to three weeks the duration of Europe–India travel, an 80 per cent drop. That ensured the pre-eminence of Bombay port over eastward-looking Calcutta and Madras. To cope with its new-found importance. Bombay established its Port Trust and reclaimed the land between Colaba and Sewri where the docks still sit.

The British Raj

Presiding over these changes was the most enduring legacy of the 1857 uprising: the professional, meritocratic Civil Service that took over administration of the colonies from the East India Company. One of the first of these new-breed administrators sent to Bombay, Sir Bartle Frere, also turned out to be the most visionary governor since Gerald Aungier.

Frere knocked down the obsolete Fort walls, conducted the first census (which recorded 816,562 inhabitants in 1866), inaugurated the High Court, installed public street-lighting, and memorialized himself with an oddly incongruous water-gushing statue of the Roman goddess of spring, which remains the main downtown landmark — the celebrated Flora Fountain.

Close on the heels of these innovations came tramcars (1874), India's first stock exchange (1875), an ice factory (1880), a telephone exchange (1882) and electric lamps (1882). This epoch also saw the proliferation of proud Victorian public buildings, culminating in the grand architectural farrago of Victoria Terminus ('VT', built in 1888), that remain Bombay's pride.

The Indian National Congress

About the same time, Bombay witnessed the creation of another sort of monument that has proved as eclectic and enduring as VT: the Indian National Congress. Today, the Congress has become the almost unassailable national ruling party. Its patronage network reaches into every facet of Indian life — a far cry from the well-meaning, but rather irrelevant talk-shop it must have seemed at its inaugural meeting in 1885.

The 72 founding delegates of the Indian National Congress reflected the cream of Bombay's cosmopolitan intellectual elite: English liberals, wily Parsi barristers, Hindu revivalists, Muslim reformists, firebrand pamphleteers. It required all the genius of no less a saint than Mohandas K Gandhi to galvinize this debating society into a mass-based national independence movement (see page 38).

Bombay since Independence

Independence for India was finally granted at midnight on 14–15 August 1947. The creation of a separate Pakistan at the same time plunged the subcontinent into virtual civil war, as confrontations between uprooted Hindus and Muslims exploded into bloody violence. Although far enough from the Indo-Pakistan border to be spared the worst of the bloodbath, Bombay became first port of call for the wave of Hindu refugees fleeing from Pakistan's southern province of Sind. These migrations further enhanced the city's commercial dynamism, as the Sindhis proved to be an exceptionally enterprising community with far-flung international links.

Dynamism, however, proved to be a mixed blessing in an India newly converted to Nehruvian socialism. With strict licensing, tight foreign exchange, import controls and marginal tax rates over 90 per cent, entrepreneurship was driven underground into a parallel economy. Bombay quickly emerged as a Mecca for 'black' money. This tidal wave of unaccounted cash found outlets in real estate speculation, the production of flashy cinema musicals, political ward-heeling and conspicuous consumption.

Bombay's fast and loose reputation soon attracted new waves of economic migrants from villages all over India. The city's population has more than doubled since Independence. Ill-conceived building codes and rent control laws have made for deteriorating old buildings, gimcrack new ones and a gross undersupply of housing. Sidewalk sleepers and jerry-built kerbside slums choked downtown streets, while sprawling shanty-towns engulfed the suburbs.

Established Bombayites, both the middle class and the industrial proletariat in the declining textile mills, felt increasingly threatened by the newcomers. Some of this resentment found articulation in the form of Marathi chauvinism, which erupted in language riots in the late '50s and early '60s. The old Bombay Presidency was carved into two linguistic states, Gujarat and Maharashtra. The latter state now has its capital in Bombay city.

Yet, despite the crush, Bombay remains one of the world's safest cities. It is a veritable museum of Victorian architecture. And a crowd-watcher's delight, not just for its diversity but also for the civility of its people. It is a city of unparalleled amenity and opportunity — the 'Urbs Primus in Indus' (First City in India), as proclaimed in its British-bequeathed motto.

A mural housed in the Bank of India's headquarters

Getting To, From and Around Bombay

Getting There

Any trip to India can be made much more enjoyable with some preparation and forethought. Even a small amount of advance information on what to expect will help you cope with the inevitable problems of a journey undertaken in a country where existing facilities are overstrained by a huge population and rapid urban growth.

By Air

Bombay's air links are at present the weak point of the transport set-up. International flights often arrive at unsociable hours (in the pre-dawn for instance) when jetlagged passengers are tired, vulnerable and least able to cope. Travelling within India can also have its drawbacks when the demand for seats on a train, plane or bus exceeds availability.

For most travellers the inconvenience of Bombay's air schedules is unavoidable; but if you can, try to work Bombay into the middle of your itinerary and schedule your arrival and departure from the country via other gateways. Buying tickets within India is best done through a reliable travel agent.

Bombay is connected by international flights to most cities in the Far East, the subcontinent, the Middle East, Europe and East Africa. The majority of long-haul flights still arrive at its Sahar International Airport between midnight and 6 am, but an increasing number of airlines are introducing evening departures from Europe, allowing for a more convenient morning arrival. All the major international airlines fly to Bombay, except JAL, KLM and Thai which all have excellent services to and through Delhi.

Air India has the greatest number of flights into Bombay with frequent evening departures from London, Amsterdam, Paris, Frankfurt and Rome, in addition to daily morning departures from London which originate in New York the previous evening.

British Airways is the most frequent European carrier into Bombay and has connections to Hong Kong and Beijing. Among the other carriers with frequent flights to and from Europe are Aeroflot, Air Canada (originating in Toronto), Air France, Alitalia, Iberia, Lufthansa, Pan Am, Qantas, Sabena, Swissair, TWA and Yugoslav.

The Middle-Eastern and Gulf carriers, such as Egypt Air, Emirates, Gulf Air, Iraqi, Kuwait and Saudi fly into Bombay and all have connections to and from most European cities. From Southeast Asia and beyond, Bombay is connected by Air India, Air Canada, Qantas and Singapore Airlines. The South Asian carriers Air Lanka,

ખોજાતી
સુરમા
KHOJATI
SURMA
AL-HAFIZ & BROS
SANJARY TRAVEL & TOURS
FLY DUBAI

Biman Bangladesh and PIA all fly into Bombay, as do Air Mauritius, Air Tanzania, Ethiopian, Kenya Airways and Zambia Airways from Africa.

On Arrival

On arrival in India the first delay any traveller experiences is the immigration queue. Baggage handling, usually slowed down by the x-ray scrutiny of all in-bound checked-in baggage, can take up to an hour after the flight has landed. However, passing through customs is usually a quick and painless experience.

There are bank counters inside the arrival terminal and money can be changed at bank rates while you are waiting for your baggage to appear.

Outside the arrival hall, there are various counters offering car rental, transfer buses and pre-paid taxis. The system of pre-paid taxis, operated by the local police, curbs any unscrupulous driver from taking an exhausted visitor on an involuntary ride through the back streets to inflate the meter charges. The taxi rates are fixed and a receipt is issued detailing the destination zone and any baggage. (In early 1989 the fare from the airport to the Gateway of India, for instance, was around Rs120.) The receipt is handed to the driver when the destination is reached. This system also works from the domestic terminals and other major airports in the country. If travelling on a budget, you may want to use the EATS bus service, which costs only a few rupees and connects the airport with most of the nearby and downtown hotels.

Domestic Flights

Bombay has two airport terminals at opposite ends of the same runway system. The international airport is locally known as Sahar and is further from the city centre. The domestic terminal, five kilometres (three miles) closer to town, is known as Santa Cruz. Santa Cruz is a major hub in both the large domestic carrier Indian Airlines network and the more recent 'third-level' airline Vayudoot. Indian Airlines has frequent connections each day with Airbus flights to and from Bangalore, Calcutta, Dabolim (Goa), Hyderabad, Madras, New Delhi and Trivandrum.

Regular Indian Airlines Boeing 737 flights connect Bombay with 25 or more stations within India. Vayudoot was established in the mid-'80s and flies smaller Avros HS748 and Dornier 228 on feeder routes, connecting Bombay with many smaller towns that are not served by Indian Airlines.

Both domestic carriers have a mixed reputation for reliability and schedules. Many flights have long waiting lists and the shortage of aircraft is made worse when more than a routine number are taken out for their regular servicing. Indian Airlines has a dual fare structure; a higher dollar tariff is applicable to all travel by foreign nationals even if the ticket is purchased in India. Air India's many offices abroad sell tickets on Indian Airlines. Reconfirmation of an international flight reservation, as well as on bookings for internal sectors, is vital. Being waitlisted is unsatisfactory whatever the promises made by the reservation staff. If travelling beyond Goa and Aurangabad (for Ajanta and Ellora), check out the variety of discount fares on Indian Airlines such as Youth Fares and the US$400 Discover India Fare allowing unlimited travel for 21 days.

Transferring from an international arrival straight through to a connecting domestic flight is most simply done by means of one of the occasional transfer buses or pre-paid taxi (see above). Overnight transit passengers who do not want to go into the city are offered a number of airport hotels. The best and most expensive is the Leela Kempinski, near Sahar. The Centaur Hotel is a few hundred metres from the domestic terminal. Both hotels operate courtesy coaches to and from all terminals at both airports. Most of the other hotels near the airport are cheaper, but cannot be recommended.

Departure

Most international flights ask you to check in two to three hours in advance — a worthwhile inconvenience if the security works. For domestic flights reporting time is 60 to 90 minutes in advance.

An airport tax of Rs300 is charged at the check-in counter for all foreign travel, except to the neighbouring countries of Afghanistan, Bangladesh, Bhutan, Burma, Maldives, Nepal and Sri Lanka when the tax is Rs150.

Intercity Rail Services

As an alternative to internal flights, try the Western Railway (headquartered at Churchgate) for Delhi and the north, Gujarat and Rajasthan; or the Central Railway out of Victoria Terminus (VT) for Calcutta, Hyderabad and other points to the east and south, respectively. Fixed price Indrail Passes are a bargain for foreign tourists and non-resident Indians. They are sold for intervals ranging from a week to three months. Tourist assistance officers at both railroads can help you with reservations from specially allotted quotas. They will also sell you copies of the *Pan-India Trains at a Glance* timetable, which can help you plan your journey in easy overnight segments.

First- and airconditioned-class sleepers are quite comfortable for overnight journeys. The crack trains are (from Bombay Central station) the Rajdhani to Delhi and the Gujarat Mail to Ahmedabad. From VT the key trains are the Deccan Queen to Pune, the Calcutta Mail via Nagpur and the Minar Express to Hyderabad.

You can depart Bombay in the evening and arrive at these convenient and interesting stopover points by the following morning. There, the railways' tourist assistance staff will help you to book your onward passage, usually involving another overnight train to the next tourist destination.

Getting Around

Although Bombay is longer than it is wide, the city seems pleasantly compact, easy to find your way around and to move about in. In the Fort area many of the major attractions, some of the main hotels and company offices are all within walking distance of each other. Entering the city from the airport can take well over an hour during the morning rush (or slow moving crush), but at other times of the day it is reasonably quick.

There is a good suburban train service, but it is only recommended outside the rush hour. East-coast commuter trains leave from Victoria Terminus (VT). Churchgate is the starting point for the west-coast trains which stop at Santa Cruz and Andheri, a short taxi ride from the domestic and international airports. Trains on both lines run every few minutes from 5 am to midnight.

Within the city, taxis are the most convenient way to get around. Although taxi fares have been increased over the years, the meters have not been brought up to date, so you actually pay a multiple of what the meter shows. In early 1989, for every rupee on the meter Rs3.75 had to be paid. All drivers have a chart showing the revised prices. In the suburbs, auto-rickshaws are available and the mark-up factor is 2.5.

Drivers sometimes balk at destinations they consider either too short or too out of the way to be profitable. If you are turned down by too many drivers, the best tactic is either to offer a premium or stage a sit-down strike in the backseat.

Cars with drivers can be hired through travel agents and hotels. Self-drive cars are not available for hire; in any case, for many visitors, a chauffeur-driven car for short-distance travel within a city is an affordable luxury in India. The rates vary with car type (air-conditioned or not, imported or local), the number of days it is wanted and so on. It is worth getting more than one quotation. For upwards of Rs200 a day, a car hired for a full day (eight hours) to visit the suburbs will often work out cheaper than a taxi. A good driver is worth tipping at the end of your stay.

The BEST bus service in the city, run by the Bombay Electrical Supply and Transport Company, operates routes to most areas. As with the trains, it is advisable to avoid the rush hours. Bus route details are on sale in downtown news kiosks.

Horse-drawn cabriolets (called 'victorias') also ply downtown streets and can be hired, with some haggling, for roughly twice what a taxi would cost over the equivalent distance. The victorias are barred from the business districts (Fort and Nariman Point) during office hours, and from the seaside Marine Drive during rush hours, but run round-the-clock in Colaba and Kalbadevi.

Markets and Shopping

Despite its growth, Bombay's commercial map still looks like a village. True, there are a few fashionable shopping centres in the fancier high-rise and hotel districts, and each neighbourhood does have its own produce market. But most vendors of any particular line of merchandise are still concentrated in their own specialized district. Thus, for hardware you go to Lohar (tinkers') Bazaar, for jewellery to Zaveri (goldsmiths') Bazaar, for fish to Sassoon Docks and so forth.

This might have made sense when the city was more compact and transportation so undeveloped that making any purchase was an all-day project rather than part of a multi-purpose shopping trip or an errand in the lunch hour. Nowadays, however, the persistence of these 'product ghettoes' works to nobody's advantage.

Buyers must still travel to out-of-the-way speciality bazaars. But sellers also lose out since the concentration of purveyors of the same product makes it easier for customers to compare prices and quality, haggle prices down and play off vendors against each other. Indian retailers' beggar-thy-neighbour instincts seem to get the better of their propensity to collude, at least at the bazaar level.

All this is good news for the tourist who enjoys scouting around town. Bombay offers bargains on such items as textiles, high-fashion casual wear, leathergoods, brass- and copperware, spices, incense, dried fruits, second-hand books, old photographs, clocks and watches and assorted bric-a-brac.

You can take advantage of the over-concentrated product ghettoes to claw back part of the 'tax' local vendors naturally load onto the prices they quote to unwary foreigners. All it takes is a little bargaining technique. A couple of pointers: when offered a price, come back with a counter-offer of half and work your way back up from there. Always try more than one vendor to establish a price range.

The Begging Bowl

he lama strode out, head high in air, and pausing an instant before the great statue of a Bodhisat in meditation, brushed through the turnstiles.

Kim followed like a shadow. What he had overheard excited him wildly. This man was entirely new to all his experience, and he meant to investigate further, precisely as he would have investigated a new building or a strange festival in Lahore city. The lama was his trove, and he purposed to take possession. Kim's mother had been Irish too.

The old man halted by Zam-Zammah and looked round till his eye fell on Kim. The inspiration of his pilgrimage had left him for a while, and he felt old, forlorn, and very empty.

'Do not sit under that gun,' said the policeman loftily.

'Huh! Owl! ' was Kim's retort on the lama's behalf. 'Sit under that gun if it please thee. When didst thou steal the milk-woman's slippers, Dunnoo?'

That was an utterly unfounded charge sprung on the spur of the moment, but it silenced Dunnoo, who knew that Kim's clear yell would call up legions of bad bazar boys if need arose.

'And whom didst thou worship within?' said Kim affably, squatting in the shade beside the lama.

'I worshipped none, child. I bowed before the Excellent Law.'

Kim accepted this new God without emotion. He knew already a few score.

'And what dost thou do?'

'I beg. I remember now it is long since I have eaten or drunk. What is the custom of charity in this town? In silence, as we do of Tibet, or speaking aloud?'

'Those who beg in silence starve in silence,' said Kim, quoting a native proverb. The lama tried to rise, but sank back again, sighing for his disciple, dead in far-away Kulu. Kim watched—head to one side, considering and interested.

'Give me the bowl. I *know the people of this city—all who are charitable. Give, and I will bring it back filled.'*

Simply as a child the old man handed him the bowl.

'Rest, thou. I know the people.'

He trotted off to the open shop of a kunjri*, a low-caste vegetable-seller, which lay opposite the belt-tramway line down the Motee Bazar. She knew Kim of old.*

'Oho, hast thou turned yogi *with thy begging-bowl? she cried.*

'Nay,' said Kim proudly. 'There is a new priest in the city—a man such as I have never seen.'

'Old priest—young tiger,' said the woman angrily. 'I am tired of new priests! They settle on our wares like flies. Is the father of my son a well of charity to give to all who ask?'

'No,' said Kim. 'Thy man is rather yagi *(bad-tempered) than* yogi *(a holy man). But this new priest is new. The Sahib in the Wonder House has talked to him like a brother. O my mother, fill me this bowl. He waits.'*

'That bowl indeed! That cow-bellied basket! Thou hast as much grace as the holy bull of Shiv. He has taken the best of a basket of onions already, this morn; and forsooth, I must fill thy bowl. He comes here again.'

The huge, mouse-coloured Brahmini bull of the ward was shouldering his way through the many-coloured crowd, a stolen plantain hanging out of his mouth. He headed straight for the shop, well knowing his privileges as a sacred beast, lowered his head, and puffed heavily along the line of baskets ere making his choice. Up flew Kim's hard little heel and caught him on his moist blue nose. He snorted indignantly, and walked away across the tram-rails, his hump quivering with rage.

'See! I have saved more than the bowl will cost thrice over. Now, mother, a little rice and some dried fish atop—yes, and some vegetable curry.'

A growl came out of the back of the shop, where a man lay.

'He drove away the bull,' said the woman in an undertone.

'It is good to give to the poor.' She took the bowl and returned it full of hot rice.

'But my yogi *is not a cow,' said Kim gravely, making a hole with his fingers in the top of the mound. 'A little curry is good, and a fried cake, and a morsel of conserve would please him, I think.'*

'It is a hole as big as thy head,' said the woman fretfully. But she filled it, none the less, with good, steaming vegetable curry, clapped a fried cake atop, and a morsel of clarified butter on the cake, dabbed a lump of sour tamarind conserve at the side; and Kim looked at the load lovingly.

'That is good. When I am in the bazar the bull shall not come to this house. He is a bold beggar-man.'

'And thou?' laughed the woman. 'But speak well of bulls. Hast thou not told me that some day a Red Bull will come out of a field to help thee? Now hold all straight and ask for the holy man's blessing upon me. Perhpas, too, he knows a cure for my daughter's sore eyes. Ask him that also, O thou Little Friend of all the World.'

But Kim had danced off ere the end of the sentence, dodging pariah dogs and hungry acquaintances.

Rudyard Kipling, Kim, *1901*

And when you threaten to 'walk away', be prepared to follow up on it. Even if you come away empty-handed, Bombay bazaar-hopping is worth it just for the sake of street-theatre. Each of the major markets is a self-contained world, with its own guild halls, temples or mosques, cafés and food stalls, protection-racketeers, elder arbiters and assorted subcontractors. A few of the more notable ones:

Chor Bazaar, or 'thieves' market'. Vendors here give out the story that the label is actually a libellous corruption of the original name 'shor bazaar', or 'noisy market'. Such a tag would certainly be justified by the prevailing din on any Friday, when junk-dealers, with their push carts, cry out their wares on Mutton Street.

Friday is the only time that casual shoppers can hope for any bargains at Chor Bazaar, and then too only on downmarket gewgaws. The rest of the week, the established antique shops (themselves no more than evolved junk-dealers) stock very pricey wares for the benefit of diplomats, multinational executives, high-rolling tourists and visiting oil sheikhs.

The stock includes a sizeable proportion of very convincing fakes. Still, the best of India's genuine antiques also find their way here, since brokers give Bombay first preference on their finds. The network is well developed and professional, with detailed descriptions and photographs widely circulated to potential buyers.

Since the 1970s, laws have prohibited export of anything older than 100 years, so most of Chor Bazaar's offerings run to Victoriana: chamberpots, stained glass cupolas, solar topees, wicker garden furniture, the whole musty attic of the Raj. Down-at-heel Parsi families used to be the main source. But now that this vein has been nearly exhausted and the dealers' net is cast wider, the market is taking on a more 'oriental' character.

You can still get good bargains at Chor Bazaar if you buy in bulk. Dealers like to keep all their distress sales 'within the trade' so as not to undercut the retail market, but at the same time they are keen to open up new overseas outlets. And if you have particular expertise in any special type of antique, chances are you know more than the still-developing antique dealers of Bombay.

For instance, undervalued Ming and Qing (Ch'ing) porcelain still crops up from time to time thanks to the Macau–Goa connection. It commands the same price as mass-produced Chinese and Japanese export wares, since nobody on Mutton Street can read Chinese kiln marks. Make the most of it while you can.

Chor Bazaar has an annex selling car parts, which perhaps helped it earn its unsavoury reputation: reportedly, if you park too close to Mutton Street, you can buy back your hubcaps, mirrors and windshield wipers at just a third of their original cost. But this is not a bad place to scout if you have an antique car back home. Smaller and cheaper 'Chor Bazaars' are also to be found in Mahim and Santa Cruz.

Crawford Market is so dramatic it is almost like a movie set — sort of a cross between Merchant Ivory and Cecil B De Mille. The place is as huge and as echoing as Victoria Terminus (which it sits right next to, at the corner of Hornby and Carnac roads). It is principally a fresh produce market, but on a massive, wholesale scale.

So, where your neighbourhood market would feature neat little piles of, say, apples, at Crawford Market they are heaped up in mountains. The same goes for every kind of produce, from cabbages to lemons to onions. Market men perch on platforms at various levels in the pile, doling out the produce by the basketful.

They virtually live there, sleeping on the same little shelves during the heat of the day and working feverishly in the cool pre-dawn. Coolies, striking in their bright white *dhotis* against the multi-coloured walls of produce, scurry about with bathtub-sized baskets on their heads.

The floor is slimy with the accumulated compost of generations. Shafts of sunlight filter in through skylights in the three-storey-high cantilevered roof; swallows and sparrows careen about. Other fauna include India's ubiquitous crows and some of the fattest rats in town.

At the hub of the market is a fountain by Lockwood Kipling (Rudyard's father, who also sculpted the bas-reliefs over the main entrances). It represents India's four major rivers and is said to be very beautiful, but is now almost always smothered in great heaps of mangoes, pineapples or whatever fruits happen to be in season.

Behind the fountain is a clutch of stands selling pets of all kinds: pert little bulbuls, cockatoos, mynas, parrots, puppies, guppies, angelfish, pirhanas, quails (and their eggs as a sideline), tortoises, bunnies, squirrels, monkeys and lots more. The Crawford Market complex has other speciality bazaars, too. There is a meat market that sells mutton and beef. The fish market is across the street. Live chickens, geese and pheasants feature in the poultry market.

Another section stocks cane and bamboo ware. The dry goods market sells crockery, hardware and stoves. The tobacco market displays more ways of preparing the weed than you might have thought possible, variously cut, cured and perfumed for sniffing and chewing, as well as smoking. A sub-section specializes in fittings for hookahs.

The smugglers' bazaar at Crawford Market specializes in comestibles spirited off the ships moored in Bombay harbour. There is the usual complement of Coca-Cola, foreign toiletries, chocolates and cheeses (all of which are either legally barred or prohibitively taxed in

AAJ-KE-SHOLEY
Door-Desh

Street-side stores sell products ranging from comics and posters (left) to soap, eggs, bread and biscuits (below)

India). But the smugglers' market features more exotic items as well, such as assorted seaweeds, teas and condiments stolen from Japanese and Korean vessels. Vendors sometimes sell very expensive delicacies for just a few rupees, simply because they are not familiar with the items and cannot read the packages.

Sassoon Docks in Colaba is the nautical equivalent of Crawford Market — a sprawling, wholesale market that will interest the tourist as much for viewing as for buying. It caters mainly to the wholesale trade, although a few vendors can be persuaded to sell their wares retail on an *ad hoc* basis.

Mornings around 8 am and afternoons around 4 pm, the place is a swarm of activity. Coolies teeter up and down gangplanks at a trot, lugging twice their own weight in fish. Light shimmers off everything — flanks of giant sharks, heaps of smelts, ice blocks, pennants on the boats, the becalmed water of the sheltered harbour.

Koli fishwives, their gaudy saris tucked up skintight around their legs, haggle noisily with customers. Sweat-slicked carters trundle fish-laden barrows through the dense crowds. The stench of fresh-fish guts is underlaid with the sharper tang of drying Bombay duck, which festoons the spars of the boats.

Tourists be warned: it is technically illegal to photograph Sassoon Docks, lest your snapshots fall into the hands of Pakistani frogmen.

For retail purchases of fish, your best bets are Colaba Market and Byculla. Dried fish — including Bombay duck — are specialities of Shewri and Grant Road markets.

For sheer profusion of merchandise, the **Muslim markets** in the southern end of Byculla are the most impressive in town. **Abdul Rehman Street** and the nearby **Jamma Bazaar** are the places to go for luxury goods like perfumes, fine muslin cloth, marbled paper and other fancy stationery, dried fruits and nuts, fine-woven straw mats and more. Right next door are the more workaday markets of **Lohar Street** and **Null Bazaar** for pipe fittings, paints, picture frames, electrical goods, cutlery and crockery.

Mohammed Ali Road sells brassware and copperware, tenting and tarpaulins and weights and measures. Its main claim to fame, though, is its congregation of night-time food stalls during the Muslim fasting month of Ramadan. **Bhendi Bazaar** features all manner of biscuits and snacks, as well as areca nuts and the various other fixings for *paan* (see page 65).

Commercial Bombay is a town built above all by the textile industry, and **Kalbadevi** has one of its oldest and biggest cloth bazaars. Natural fibre fabrics — wool, silk, cotton — are well made and good value, and likeliest to attract foreigners. Locals, on the other hand, seem to get more excited nowadays about synthetics or blends, as witness the energetic bargaining over suit- and sari-lengths in the *kapida-wallahs*' stalls.

For **handwoven textiles**, something of a fetish in India thanks to Mahatma Gandhi's advocacy, try the government-run **Khadi Emporium** on D N Road, or the private boutiques off **Sir P M Road** in the Fort district.

Cricketers and field-hockey players can load up on gear in the **sporting goods** shops around **Dhobi Talao**, one of the city's main Goan ghettoes. This neighbourhood also features a few pork butchers, a rarity elsewhere in Bombay as in most of India. Reportedly, if you know where to look, you can even find homemade wine and *feni* (white lightning made of coconuts or cashews) around here, a legacy of the days when Goan 'aunties' used to alleviate the thirst of prohibition-parched Bombay.

Old-time photo shops near Dhobi Talao sometimes come up with rare treasures for specialist collectors: antique cameras, glass negatives, hand-tinted photo-portraits and the like.

Cotton casuals destined for European and American markets somehow find their way instead to **Fashion Street**, a stretch of Cross Maidan opposite the Bombay Gymkhana, where they sell at a fraction of what they would cost in Western deparment stores. A lot of the merchandise is factory 'seconds', so double-check for small defects. But with due vigilance, you can outfit yourself on the cheap in the latest foreign fashions and augment your store of lightweight, easily washed cotton clothes for your Indian sojourn.

Fashion Street also sells handbags, heavy costume jewellery and other accessories. After you have decked yourself out in punkish chic, you can top off the whole ensemble with a skinhead haircut for Rs3 from one of the kerbside barbers at the end of the row of stalls.

Leatherworkers, traditionally low-caste Muslims, have grown rich within the past few years by almost faultlessly imitating designer **footwear, luggage** and **leather accessories**. Their wares may be pricey by Indian standards, but still cost a fraction of what you would pay for 'originals' in Europe, America or Japan. The main places to look for these items are in **Crawford Market**, **Null Bazaar**, behind Bhendi Bazaar, and on **Colaba Causeway** near the Regal Cinema.

Books, new and old, can be bought off the kerbside along the stretch of **Churchgate Street** running from the Flora Fountain past the Central Telegraph Office to the Western Railway headquarters. Also at the 'Y' **intersection of Mahatma Gandhi Road** and **Hornby Road**. Half the stock is remaindered American titles. They sell for Rs5–15 for paperbacks, slightly more for fancy coffee-table picture books.

The real treasures, though, are in the second-hand category. The vendors, many of them Nepalis who do not read or speak English, acquire books in job lots from estate settlements. The volumes are often still in bales tied up with twine when they come to the kerbside market, where they are sold by the yard for shelf-fillers. You have to make your own way through the higgledy-piggledy assortment of titles.

It is often worth the effort. You could stumble upon anything from old turn-of-the-century encyclopedias to combat memoirs of Raj campaigners, abstruse textbooks to carefully hand-annotated cookbooks — all for Rs10–20 apiece. One lucky Frenchman reportedly even found a first edition of Victor Hugo.

If you prefer book shopping on less of a grab-bag basis, the **New and Second-hand Bookstore** at Kalbadevi offers a staggering range of old titles, many of them rare outside the quirky backwaters of India. And the **Strand Book Stall** off Pherozeshah Mehta Marg in the Fort has a wide selection of brand-new European and American books at discounts of 10–20 per cent, or even more for remaindered items.

Best value for new books, though, may be the Soviet-run bookstore on Warden Road or the private (and hence more accommodating, although still ideologically communist) **People's Book House** on Cowasjee Patel Street in the Fort. In their specialities — technical subjects, Russian and Marxist classics, children's fables — it is hard to

Superstar

In 1982, one of the more spectacular incidents concerning the cinema occurred in India. Amitabh Bachan, the James Dean of the Indian screen and the heartthrob of the masses, was seriously injured while shooting an action scene in a movie. He had severe abdominal injuries and was hospitalized for several weeks, fighting for his life.

The entire nation went beserk over this event. It was front-page headline news in all the papers across the country. Prime Minister Indira Gandhi canceled a foreign trip in order to visit the ailing actor in the hospital (accompanied by her son Rajiv). Prayers were offered across the land, pujas *were performed in thousands of temples, a day-and-night vigil was installed outside the hospital. Hourly bulletins were issued describing Mr. Bachan's condition, including every medical particular, ranging from the state of the lungs to fecal matter. Most of this medical history was also printed in detail in major publications.*

India prayed for a man, barely forty, who was a tough guy on the screen and could fetch the highest price that any actor has ever commanded on the Indian screen. The state of shock and prayerful hope extended far beyond the gullible masses of India. Amitabh Bachan's condition became the staple fare of cocktail-party conversation in Delhi and Bombay.

Extensive analysis was made of his character, and of the roles he might have played had he lived (it was assumed that even if he did not die, he would never again play on the screen), and all kinds of real-life fantasies were woven round a perfectly ordinary man.

When he recovered, as he was bound to do, because good guys never die in any good film, billboards went up thanking God and various other deities who had been called into action to save this precious life. For days on end, there was jubilation on the streets, and the prime minister made a special reference to this epoch-making medical turnaround in the Indian Parliament. Short of canonization, Mr. Bachan had had the best of both life and death.

Sasthi Brata, India: Labyrinths in the Lotus Land

beat the Soviets for publishing quality, especially at the giveaway prices offered in consideration of India's cozy relationship with Moscow.

Eats

Like any other big, rich city, Bombay has the usual complement of five-star hotel restaurants serving Continental specialities. The standard Mughlai and Punjabi fares are also widely available in middle-class restaurants. And what is left of the Chinese community can still turn out better-than-average food in any of a dozen old establishments. Continental, generic Indian and Chinese restaurants are listed on pages 182–7.

Upmarket new joints are continually opening in all three of these types. Decor is considerably snazzier than before, and even the food is quite respectable in some of them. But they have nothing that you would not find anywhere else Indian yuppies might congregate.

There are a few dishes that are peculiar to Bombay, though. And the pursuit of these delights can bring you into contact with some of the city's more colourful districts and people. For example, why not try:

Dhansak, a Parsi speciality. The basic ingredient is split lentils, or *dhal*, the staple protein source of the Indian vegetarian diet. But the Parsi innovation is to stew it in a special *masala* with chicken or mutton. The result can be pretty grim in the average Irani café version. But it is something special at a few choice spots like the Paradise on Colaba Causeway, or Dorabjee's Ram Punjab on Ambedkar Road.

Goan dishes (see page 193) are served at Martin's, near Strand Cinema in Colaba, Sacru Menezes on D'Mello Road in the Fort District and a host of small establishments near Dhobi Talao.

Gujarati *thalis*, the all-you-can-eat vegetarian platters in the sweetish style of Maharashtra's neighbouring state. Widespread in Bombay, these restaurants are more of a rarity outside of Western India. Famous *thalis* are served at Rajdhani, near Crawford Market; Rasna and Purohit near Churchgate; Aram in Mahim; and Thacker's Club on Marine Drive.

Pao Bhajii, a puffy flatbread stuffed with vegetable curry and deep fried. Street food at its greasy best, it is the Bombay equivalent of pizza — a kerbside meal unto itself for Rs6 or less, popular with students and clerks.

Mutton mince is the staple for all meals in Muslim teashops. One hole-in-the-wall (literally embedded in the side of the Jamma Masjid) is reputed to have learned its secret heirloom recipe from an angel disguised as a beggar. Almost as divine is the mutton mince served at the Olympia Hotel on Colaba Causeway.

Beef items, usually shunned by the cow-venerating Hindus, are eaten with relish in the Muslim areas of Byculla. Trotters are the speciality at Saat Hamdi and Barah Hamdi on Mohammed Ali Road. For beef marrow try Gulshan-e-Iran near Crawford Market and a string of restaurants opposite the telephone exchange on Miyan Ahmed Street.

Kebabs somehow taste better eaten alfresco. Bombay's finest are at Do Tankii, an illegal hawkers' stand directly under a bought-off police *chowki* on Maulana Shaukatali Road. There you can stuff yourself to bursting for barely Rs10 per head.

The kebabs come with sizzling hot *parathas* (an oily kind of flatbread), mint leaves, chopped onions and lemons, all served in generous and replenishable piles. Fat sheep wander about among the diners, but the meat used turns out to be beef.

The place is thick with beggars — amputees, lepers, *chadoor*-draped Muslim widows — but they discreetly wait until after you have finished dining and paying before they apply for leftover scraps and change. Foreigners should bring their own supply of boiled water. Although tables are provided, you can also drive up in your own car or a taxicab and eat inside the vehicle; recommended for unaccompanied women.

More relaxed, if a bit less fresh and generous in its offerings, is Burre Miyan's outdoor kebabery on Apollo Street, behind the Taj. This place has the added advantage of a retail wine shop close at hand, where you can buy beer to wash down your feast. The kebabs at Bachchu ki Wadi on Shuklaji Street also come recommended.

Kulfi, the milk-rich local variant of ice cream, features on the dessert menus of most local restaurants, but is best savoured in street-side stalls. Sold by the 100-gram (3½-ounce) portion (weighed out on elaborate brass scales), it comes in a bewildering profusion of flavours ranging from *malai* (plain cream) through a variety of *pistas* (nuts) and tropical fruits like *chikoo*, *sitaphal* (custard apple), pineapple and mango.

A pair of famous *kulfi* stands draw crowds to the corner where Sandhurst Road (now renamed Vallabhbhai Patel Road) meets Chowpatty. One of the two, the Parsi Dairy Farm, is a branch of a chain that has its main *kulfi* parlour on Princess Street.

Kulfi sundaes with various syrups, nuts and *sevaian* (a kind of vermicelli) are concocted in sweet shops like Kailash Parbhat on Third Pasta Lane in Colaba or Badshah's opposite Crawford Market. But the best *kulfi*, purists swear, is dished out by the pushcarts behind Mumbadevi Temple.

Bhel puri, the quintessential Bombay snack, a savoury mixture of puffed rice, deep fried vermicelli, chopped onions and potatoes. It is garnished with a dash of lemon, some fresh coriander and dollops of chutney (a high-octane combination of coriander, mint, ginger and garlic). The whole hodgepodge is scooped up with little fried flatbreads about the size of a biscuit.

Everywhere in the city you will find *bhel puri* stands, with the various ingredients displayed in colourful piles on a background of bright red bunting. Chowpatty beach has a concentration of them, brightly lit up at night. So has Juhu and Malabar Hill in front of the Hanging Gardens.

Channa, or nuts of various kinds, are sold by vendors who carry an assortment on a tray slung around their necks. You can choose between groundnuts and garbanzos flavoured with many different salt-and-spice mixtures. The *channa-wallah* will warm up your selection under a small, portable charcoal brazier and serve it in a twisted paper cone. Another kerbside speciality, especially during the monsoon season, is baked maize (corn) garnished with lemon and chilli.

Bombay duck — do not be put off by the smell. This salty dried fish snack has rightly projected the fame of the humble Kolis, repeated around the world. Rumour has it that deep-fried Bombay duck has shown up on the bar-counters of some of the most exclusive clubs in London and New York. You can buy the same stuff much cheaper and fresher in virtually any produce market in town. Colaba Market, Sassoon Docks, Mazgaon and Crawford Market offer a particularly wide selection. The only hitch is that you will have to cook it for yourself; Bombay bars and restaurants, curiously enough, do not serve it ready-made.

Konkan cuisine is naturally long on seafood, reflecting the cove-studded coast that is home to the largest single bloc of Bombay's industrial proletariat. The only time to be a little wary of this food is during the monsoon, when rough weather keeps the fishing fleet from venturing far enough to reach pollution-free waters, while rain-flush drainage systems discharge their year's accumulation into the bay.

Crabs, shrimp, pomfret, baby clams, even eels figure on the menu at places like Saayba's in Santa Cruz. Sindudurg Hotel in Dadar often attracts long queues for its famous seafood *thalis*, especially after rallies of the Marathi-chauvinist Shiv Sena party in nearby Shivaji Park (where Bombay's mayor lives).

Most of these dishes tend to be heavy, featuring rich and spicy sauces or else deep-fried fish. Aside from chopped onions, vegetables seem almost unheard of in this cuisine.

Fresh seafood is better sought at Bombay's top-line Chinese

وما بكم من نعمة فمن الله
اور تمہارے پاس جو کچھ بھی نعمت ہے وہ سب اللہ ہی کی طرف سے ہے

restaurants such as Kamling's on Vir Nariman Road, the Mandarin and Nanking (just opposite one another on Apollo Pier Road). They have the good sense not to overcook Bombay's rich seasonal harvest of giant blue crabs, pomfret, sea bass, tiger prawns and the like.

Just ask the waiter what is fresh at the moment and order it steamed with black beans or poached with ginger and scallions. During the monsoon, it is best to avoid seafood altogether. A few of the pretentious newer Chinese restaurants in ritzy locations like Kemp's Corner serve not-so-fresh seafood, heavily doused with monosodium glutemate and outrageously priced.

Juice bars like Badshah's near Crawford Market or Kailash Parbhat in Colaba offer fresh-pressed custard apple, *chikoo*, pomegranate, mango, *mosambi*, tomato and lots more. Some of the best of these are nameless, like the Irani joint on Gunbow Street in the Fort (near the Bombay Mutual Building) or the kerbside stand on Chowpatty seaface opposite the Flotilla Restaurant.

Paan, the local version of betel, makes an ideal conclusion for a Bombay blow-out meal. You might feel more comfortable about trying it in India, versus the Chinese or Malay regions (where betel is also eaten), since the narcotic and addictive properties of the areca nut are neutralized in subcontinental preparations by boiling it first in milk.

The basic preparation is to wrap areca in a betel leaf that has been daubed with lime. This is the recipe for *sada* (or plain) *paan*. Even the no-frills product, though, is subject to lots of variation: the leaf can be the tender local version or the coarser, more flavourful, *bangla*. The *supari* (nut) can be chopped, shaved or shredded, pre-soaked or dried and so on.

When you venture into *mita* (sweet) *paan*, even more possibilities open up. The vendor may add *gulkhand* (a kind of mildly laxative marmalade), rose syrup, menthol, tulsi leaves, cumin seeds, cardamom, cloves and more. All these condiments are kept in an array of mysterious brass vessels on a giant platter, before which the cross-legged *paan-wallah* presides.

Deluxe *paan* even come iced and coated with edible gold or silver leaf. Upon request, *paan* may also be laced with tobacco or other drugs. Such concoctions can cost several rupees — the price of a working-class *thali* meal. Even the barest *sada paan* costs a rupee or so. Considering the amount of tax-free turnover a *paan-wallah* can do in a day, the business is potentially very profitable.

Paan is available on practically every street corner, but *cognoscenti* go far out of their way to visit their favourite *paan-wallahs*. For some reason, the aristocracy of the trade comprises Brahmins from Uttar Pradesh — look out for the telltale topknot, the sacred thread and, most of all, the lurid red teeth of an inveterate betel-eater.

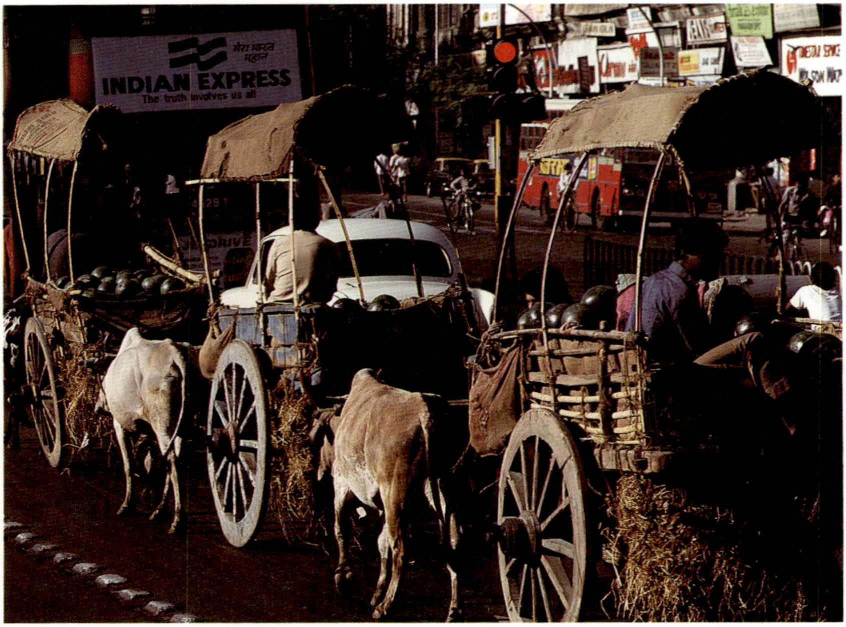
INDIAN EXPRESS
The truth involves us all

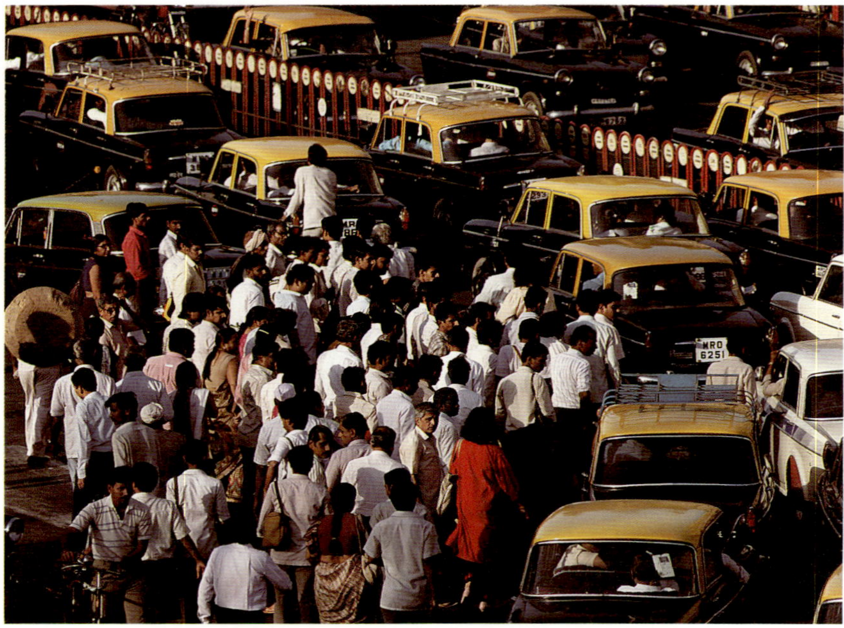

MRO
6251

Raj Kapoor

Indians call their cinema '*masala* movies', likening the film-makers' pinch-of-everything formula for box-office success to the pungent spice mixtures of the national cuisine. Yet, despite the note of self-deprecation, most Bombayites would have neither their food nor their films any other way.

And the original *masala* movie recipe was cooked up by Raj Kapoor, scion of a distinguished theatrical family. His ingredients: large dollops of sublimated eroticism, a hint of leftist ideology, plenty of glitz, song and dance, plus a wistful 'Eternal Tramp' persona likened (perhaps too often) to Charlie Chaplin's.

At the time of his commercial ascendancy, in the 1950s and '60s, Kapoor's fame spread throughout South and East Asia, the Middle East and — especially — the USSR. At first, his personal life mirrored his art, through a series of much-publicized affairs with his leading ladies.

Then, at mid-career (in the 1970s), he tried to make his art imitate his life in a four-hour autobiographical extravaganza that flopped disastrously. This setback was followed by a sequence of deaths and defections by crucial members of his writing and production team.

In a bid to pull his RK Studios out of the resulting tail-spin, Kapoor started dishing up the *masala* with a heavier hand: less ideology, more glitz and soggier saris (a turn-on for Indian audiences). It worked, sparking a whole generation of imitators, and Kapoor died rich and widely mourned in 1988 at the age of 63.

Entertainment

Bombay is by far the liveliest entertainment city in India, as a glance at the Engagements column of any daily newspaper will attest. It is the only metropolis in the country with enough going on to warrant a glossy *Time Out*-style city magazine (called *Bombay*, widely sold at news stands). But some of the liveliest and most offbeat entertainment never makes it into the printed listings. A sampling:

Theatre

Besides a sprinkling of **musicals** and **comedies** from London's West End playing virtually every week, there is the perennial production of 'Bottoms Up!', a slick (if somewhat slapstick) **cabaret** on Indian topics, updated periodically. Little theatre groups mount **avant garde plays** or **repertory classics** from abroad, sometimes very effectively staged and directed. A few of these productions feature nationally known film actors paying artistic penance for their glitzy screen extravaganzas.

The most original productions in Bombay, though, are the **Indian-language dramas**, especially in Marathi. These plays draw on a richer folk idiom, appeal to a wider audience and tackle more relevant themes. Even if you do not understand the words, the staging is powerful and often you can find someone in the audience to give you a gloss on the action.

Film

By sheer footage, Bombay is the cinema capital of the world. Most of its output comprises Hindi-language **masala movies**, so named because of their *masala* (spicy mixture) of song and dance, tear-jerking pathos, slapstick, jingoism, magic, special effects, social 'relevance', stylized titillation, villainy and heroism.

With that many ingredients, small wonder many Hindi features are nearly three hours long. Luckily, you are given an interval in the middle to find snacks and lavatories in the somewhat down-at-heel art deco splendour of the downtown **cinema palaces**.

Hindi movies are as much fun to watch in production as on the screen. A half dozen **studios** in sylvan suburban settings rent out indoor and outdoor space to production companies. To find out what is shooting where, just call up any of the film industry trade magazines like *Film City* or *Box Office*. Getting on the set is surprisingly easy: nobody stops you at the gate.

You might see the same popinjay star playing snippets of several films in a given day at the same studio. Matinée idols are in such heavy demand that they sign on literally scores of simultaneous projects. An increasing number of foreign movies are also filmed in Bombay nowadays, thanks to the Raj revival abroad.

Art films and quality imports are displayed at the Sterling Cinema near Victoria Terminus (VT) and at Bandra Talkies in Bandra. You can screen old Indian masterpieces by Satyajit Ray and others at the **film archive** in the National Centre for the Performing Arts (NCPA), if you can convince Dr Deshpande there of your research interest.

Some of the best modern art films are made in Kerala and screened every Sunday morning at the Regal Cinema in Colaba for the benefit of the local Malayali community. Films made in Indian languages other than Hindi are usually subtitled in English.

Music

More like jazz than like the classical repertory of the West, **Indian classical music** is improvisational, usually performed by a three- or four-member combo whose personnel may change from one 'set' to the next.

Although geographically removed from the heartland of both the northern (Hindustani) and southern (Carnatic) styles, Bombay today has India's biggest concentration of what has always been the lifeblood of traditional Indian music: moneyed patronage. As a result, the city now boasts its own *gharana*, or school, of music, the 'Bhendi Bazaar style'.

Bombay is also prominent on the national concert circuit, so that most major vocalists and instrumentalists come to town several times a year. Some of their appearances are high-fashion events, but just as often they offer free concerts in school halls and neighbourhood community centres.

The best concerts of all are not listed in the newspapers, but held in private homes in the classic chamber music tradition. If you are lucky, you can find out about these soirees by calling up societies like the **Indian Music Group** at St Xavier's College (which also maintains a superb **tape library** and offers a brilliant month-long **music appreciation course** every summer).

Vocal music is considered 'purer' than instrumental, with the reflective *khyal* regarded as the apex of Hindustani classicism, followed by a wide range of lighter religious or romantic forms. The melodic line is improvised around a *raga* (a mode or theme) set to a *tal* (a rhythmic cycle of up to 36 stressed and unstressed beats). Compositions pass through a set sequence of movements, with Carnatic forms somewhat more rigidly defined than Hindustani.

The two styles also differ in instrumentation, with Persian inventions like the zither more popular in the north than the south. Carnatic ensembles even incorporate clay pots as percussion instruments. Both styles readily adapt Western instruments; the violin is now quite 'Indianized', as is the harmonium, a bellows-driven keyboard instrument that has all but disappeared in the West. Mandolins, Hawaiian guitars, electric organs and harmonicas have all been tried.

On the other hand, **fusion groups** have experimented with Indian instruments, *ragas* and *tals* in a rock setting. These groups, as well as more conventional local and foreign **rock bands**, often play at the outdoor Rang Bhavan, the venue also for the world-class biannual **Jazz Yatra** festival.

Dance

Bharata Natyam, a devotional dance form that originally used to be performed only by outcaste temple prostitutes, has become fashionable with the current generation and for the daughters of rich families to study. Since Bombay enjoys India's highest concentration of rich girls, the city has become a Mecca for dance masters.

An office worker gets an ear-clean

After years of rigorous Bharata Natyam training, girls are ready for their **angaretram**, a kind of cross between a concert debut and a cotillion. These events, well publicized in the newspapers, are worth a visit both for the performance itself and for the window they offer onto Bombay society.

Seasoned dancers often present recitals not only of Bharata Natyam, but also of such forms as the statuesque **Odissi** (from Orissa) and the expressive **Mohiniyattam** (from Kerala). **Kathakali**, a highly stylized dance-drama from Kerala, is performed to a clangorous accompaniment of drums, gongs and cymbals that convey the moods and metabolic rhythms of the characters. Under the gaudy make-up, minute movements of the actors' faces and especially the eyes take on heightened significance. Sit as close as possible to the front row to catch this action.

The heavily Persian-influenced North Indian **Kathak** features dazzling percussion duets between the barefoot 'tap-dancer' and the *tabalchi* (drummer). A considerably bastardized version of this form is presented by the **Nautch Girls**, who perform for private audiences in their apartments.

The patron, nawab-style, keeps stoking the *danseuse* with money every couple of minutes: Rs5 notes in downmarket *chawls* like Congress House off Girgaum Road, Rs20 or even Rs50 in such classy precincts as Marine Drive or Neapansea Road. The more cash proffered, the more gyrations elicited.

Bars

If you like to tipple with a view, the bars atop the Taj, Oberoi and Ambassador hotels offer matchless seascapes. Just as lordly a prospect can be viewed from the terrace of the Naaz Café on Malabar Hill without paying five-star prices, but you will have to settle for beer, since few bars outside of hotels, fancy restaurants and private clubs serve any other alcoholic drinks.

The Fort and Churchgate areas have scores of pleasant little **Irani restaurants** and even a couple of sidewalk cafés where home-bound commuters stop for an afternoon beer en route to the station. **Gokuli's** in Colaba enjoys a Bohemian reputation among the college crowd. Even more downmarket are the numerous 'country liquor' shops serving toddy and home-brew.

To drink in Maharashtra, you technically need a government permit that proclaims you a confirmed alcoholic. Rare is the barkeeper that ever asks to see this document, but if you insist, a few 'permit rooms' (as Bombay bars are officially called) will sell you one over the counter for Rs12. It makes a fine souvenir.

Services

Services of the most humdrum sort may be performed with such flourish in Bombay that they rank among the lively arts in their own

Bombay's dabbawallahs *deliver hot lunches to office workers*

right. For instance, Rs5 will buy you a half-hour's monologue from a street-corner barber plus, incidentally, a complete shave, haircut, moustache trim and headrub. Pomade optional. Likewise, a full body massage on the sands of Chowpatty or Juhu costs only about Rs20 (but leave your valuables in the hotel).

For a spiritual massage, try the Hare Krishna's ashram-cum-theme-park at Juhu, the Theosophical Society on New Marine Lines or the Ananda Margis' retreat at Ganeshpuram (which also features a hot spring). The Bombay Yellow Pages list two columns of astrologers, many of whom can deliver your chart together with an entertaining spiel in English for a couple of hundred rupees.

Services of a more intimate sort are on offer in the cheap, sordid brothels of Kamathipura, where the girls perch on little shelves affixed to the house-fronts for your shopping convenience. Bombay recorded its first known AIDS death here in 1988. Upmarket girls work out of some of the classiest high-rises in town.

Highs of every description are readily available in Bombay, some of them semi-legal. Ganja (marijuana) and hashish are freely passed around among the *sadhus* (purported ascetics) that congregate in the couple of blocks between Chowpatty and Babulnath. *Paan-wallahs* (betel-nut vendors) openly sell hash around Mumbadevi Temple.

A couple of Chinese-run opium dens are rumoured still to operate around Foras Road, despite police crackdowns. This area also attracts heroin addicts in search of 'brown sugar'.

But, supposedly, the drug of choice for the truly affluent in Bombay is snake venom. Snake charmers offer a drive-in service to wealthy patrons who pull up in limousines around midnight after the last picture show at the Metro Cinema. A bite from the right kind of adder reportedly costs upwards of Rs1,000 and keeps you high for nearly four days — if you live through it.

Discos

These are so far confined to the posh hotels. The biggest and best appointed, '1900s' in the Taj, is open only to members and hotel guests. As a result, it is patronized mainly by rich kids spending daddy's money. The Oberoi's 'Cellar', equally pricey but open to all, is favoured by self-made yuppies. The discos at the Sea Rock and Holiday Inn up in Bandra cater less to socialites than to dance fanatics.

If you are not yet in that league, you might care to try a course from Bombay's legendary dance teacher, J J Rodriguez, D T A (M B) G Brit., M I D M A (B B) Lond., A M A T D (B B) Lond., Aust. The degrees were awarded after examinations by visiting Terpsichorean Academicians. He will also issue a diploma, after just ten half-hour lessons, which can be compressed into a day for jet-setters.

He will teach any steps you like — he subscribes to a London service which sends him diagrams of the latest. But he seems to specialize in the waltz, mambo, cha cha and paso doble. Only breakdance is excluded as being 'too dangerous'. Rodriguez' alumni convene at his Colaba studio every Thursday evening for a kind of social-cum-refresher course. They routinely take prizes at such annual bashes as the Goan carnival balls or the Anglo-Indian Christmas dance in the Heritage Hotel. Rodriguez maintains a bulletin board of what dances are on each week.

Sports

Horse-racing is taken so seriously that the city comes to a virtual standstill on Derby Day. In between races, you can rent a mount from the Amateur Riders Club for **horse-riding** around the Mahalaxmi Racecourse (named after the goddess of wealth and fortune).

Most Saturdays except during the monsoon, you have only to present yourself around noontime at the Royal Yacht Club next to the Taj to be taken on as a crewman in a rather beery and laid-back **sailing** race.

Traditional Indian **wrestling** is set in dried claypits near Sewri. Greased contestants dust each other with clay to get a handhold. Some purportedly sew betal nuts into their ears to rev up their fighting spirit.

Kite fights lure hundreds up to Kalyan on windy weekends. **Cock fights** can be found in the Goan enclaves near Mazgaon. Private clubs offer the usual **racquet sports** and **swimming**. Many offer guest membership for foreign visitors.

Chowpatty, day or night, is the best place to view the peculiarly yogic sport of **kabadi**, an Indian invention. This is a kind of tag game. The player who is 'it' gets to prance about behind 'enemy lines' for as long as he can keep muttering 'kabadikabadikabadi . . .' in a single breath. In the end he either faints, quits or catches an opponent.

The Legacy of the Raj

The Raj lives in downtown Bombay. It shows in the Gothic building façades, the High Court advocates in gowns and bands, the imperial lions flanking the portico of Victoria Terminus (VT), the bright red double-decker buses, the blazer-clad school children, the prim formal gardens, the fussy prose of the daily press, the down-at-heel gentility of the old private clubs (see page 80).

Visitors to Bombay can share in the city's imperial charms by taking out temporary membership or even staying in one of these grand old clubs: the **Bombay Willingdon**, the **Bombay Gymkhana**, the

An Honoured Guest

I had a pleasant experience at the Bombay Club a week or ten days later. Early one morning I arrived in the city from a long journey in the country—too early for hotel hospitality, so I thought of the club, & coffee. I got in, & got upstairs: there, in the great dining room, a detachment of turbaned & slightly-clad coolies were scrubbing the floor. They could not understand English. I tried to make them comprehend that the privileges of temporary memberships had been conferred upon me & that I would be more than grateful for a chance to excercise them—but I did not succeed. Then a native waiter appeared, & he understood me, and made me comfortable in a small breakfast room, & brought a cup of coffee & the paper. I was soon refreshened, strengthened, & ready to go. I called a passing waiter, & asked for my bill. He was gone about a minute, & came back with another cup of coffee, but brought no bill. I explained but he did not seem to get the idea. I drank the coffee and kept watch for another waiter. When I saw one he took the order for the bill, but brought another cup of coffee instead. I drank it & waited for another waiter. He went after the bill & brought another cup of coffee. And so it went on, & there was was no understanding it. When I had drank nine cups, & could not hold any more, I turned out to see if I could find a waiter who could understand me. But every time I approached one he dodged away. Then something occurred to me which should have occurred to me before: that the waiters had quite naturally taken me for an unauthorized interloper, & that they didn't know what to do with me or how to get rid of me in the absence of their officers, & had *conceived the idea of pacifying me with coffee until Providence should have pity and interfere. It was a delicate situation. It was embarrassing to stay, & it was embarrassing to try to go . On the whole, I thought I would try to go. On the stairs I came across that first waiter, & told him my trouble & asked for my bill, & said I had tried my best to make the others understand. But he said—*

"Oh, they understood!"

That was a surprise.

"They understood? Then why didn't they bring the bill."

"Oh, they had their orders—it was all right."

"What orders?"

"The President's. He told us to watch out for you, & remember your face, & said we must give you whatever you wanted & not let you pay anything, you being the guest of the club."

"I understand it, now. Well, that is very genuine hospitality. I pressed it pretty hard, but that was because I didn't know & because I couldn't seem to make the boys understand. I suppose that if I had asked for the bill, right along, say forty-five times—why then—"

He was ready, & said with a pleasantly grave face & a polite bow—

"Why then, sir I am sure you wouldn't need any more coffee today."

Mark Twain,
in a passage suppressed by his wife from Following the Equator,
1897

Cricket Club, the **Yacht Club**, the **Amateur Riding Association**. Rates are surprisingly affordable, but it takes some advance booking and introductions (see page 193). Hostelries, ranging from the five-star Taj Mahal to the 'Ys' and the Salvation Army, still also retain their Raj flavour. So do such far-flung outposts as the **Breach Candy Swimming Baths** or the **Mahalaxmi Racecourse**.

But the most concentrated dose of Victoriana is centred on the city's downtown commercial hub. Begin with a ramble round the **Fort district**, named after the long-defunct Fort George, which used to defend the harbour. The old ramparts are long gone. But in their place, a series of imperial administrators and merchant princes in the last two centuries ordained a square mile or so of self-important commercial buildings. Architectural styles range from Art Deco to Indo-Saracenic to Neo-Classical to Gothic Revival.

Depending on the season, the weather could be too hot or too wet to walk all of the circuit described here (although in winter it can be done quite comfortably). But there is a wide choice of resting spots along the way: Irani tea shops, juice bars, beer joints, South Indian coffee houses, park benches, churches. Then, too, you can always opt out by jumping into a taxi. They are plentiful throughout south Bombay, although some of the drivers might balk at unremuneratively short journeys studded with detours and waits.

A lordlier prospect of the city can be had — at least outside of rush hours — from the top deck of an omnibus. Several routes link Shyama Prasad Mukharji Chowk with Victoria Terminus (the two foci of our Fort ellipse). The number 3 route runs east of the city centre, up Shahid Bhagat Singh Road, past Elphinstone Circle and the Asiatic Society, around Ballard Pier to Nagar Chowk. The number 1 bus sweeps down the west side of the Fort along the grand crescent of Dadabhai Naoroji Road, past Flora Fountain and on to the Prince of Wales Museum. Or else, to ride in true Raj splendour, you might book one of the horse-drawn victorias that regularly ply between VT and the Gateway of India late in the evening, when the Fort area is comparatively free of its teeming crush of people and vehicles.

The **Gateway of India** and the adjacent **Taj Mahal Hotel** make a good starting (or ending) point for the Fort circuit. Built in 1913 to commemorate a royal visit, the crypto-Moresque archway welcomed the last few generations of viceroys, governors and top civil servants as they disembarked by launch from their P & O steamers.

Like as not, they checked into the grandiose quayside hostelry for a few days to recover from seasickness before proceeding upcountry. The great domed Taj, the very symbol of Raj ostentation, was paradoxically built by Parsi industrialist Jamsethji Tata to avenge the snub of being excluded from the 'whites only' hotels of 19th-century Bombay.

The picture windows of the first-floor tearoom in the Taj's old wing command a grand view of the harbour, with battleships and shore batteries exchanging gun salutes, Arab-style dhows cruising past under full sail and freighters rusting at anchor waiting for a berth at Bombay's chronically overcrowded wharves. The same prospect can be seen from the public promenade below, for those hardy enough to brave the swarm of vendors, beggars and street performers that fasten onto strolling foreigners.

Hard by the Taj stands the **Bombay Yacht Club**, whose main entrance (on Apollo Pier Road) affords a glimpse of polished brass bells and cannon, varnished ships' models, gaudy signal flags and gleaming trophies. The honorary consul of Ireland, R Leybourne Callahan-of-India (as he styles himself), keeps court here, regaling visitors with readings of his rather acerbic verse.

Beyond Mukharji Chowk, follow Mahatma Gandhi Road past the Museum. The collections are described on pages 87–90, but the Indo-Saracenic building and its formal gardens are worth a glance on this walking tour. So are the snake charmers, street barbers and cotton-garment pedlars that crowd the sidewalk near the entrance. Turn right on Rampart Row, cross to the north side of the street and plunge into the back streets along Rope Walk Lane.

At the corner of Motiwani Path and V B Gandhi Marg stands the rococo, blue-washed **Baghdadi Synagogue**. The once-flourishing, wealthy congregation of immigrants from Iraq has now been depleted, with many of its members settling in Israel or the West. But there is still a prayer quorum of old men every evening in the century-old second-storey tabernacle.

A quorum of another kind convenes every afternoon a few blocks away at Dalal Street, home of the **Bombay Stock Exchange**, where the term 'kerb market' is taken literally. The Bourse has moved into a new curvilinear skyscraper and trading has been computerized since the unprecedented equity boom of 1985. But after the all-too-brief 150 minutes of official dealing each day, the traditional *dhoti*-clad *dalals* (brokers) spill out on to the exchange steps to carry on vociferously trading stocks almost without a break — a spectacle well worth watching. Official tours of the Bourse can be arranged by calling the Exchange management (tel. 275626). The skyscraper also affords an unmatchable bird's-eye view of the business district and the adjacent port.

From ground level, the port does not offer much to see, ringed as it is with high walls along Sahid Bhagat Singh Road. The docks at this

TRAVELS
182
188
Swiss Review of World Affairs
195
INDIA
Harper's
HORIZON
59
60
61
62
63
64
65
66
67
68
69
70
72
73
74
76
77
79
80
82
83
84
86
87
88
89
90
92
93
94
95
96
97
99
105
107
110
111
THE LANCET

TRAVELS
SILENCE

Gandhi and his wife return from South Africa in 1915 (above left); House of Mahatma Gandhi (above right); National leaders with Gandhi in Delhi (below).

The Raj in Bombay

It is hardly nostalgia for colonial rule that keeps the traditions of the Raj alive in Bombay. No city was more committed than this to the independence struggle. Nor is the Raj legacy a slavish imitation of a far-off and bygone metropole. Rather, Bombay feels as much entitled to its Victoriana as any British city, having contributed more than its share to the ethos of the age. From Bombay, the Empire drew its gin, its gingham and much of its jingoism: the city, so bustling and outwardly European, came to symbolize to self-satisfied Britons the 'progressive' face of colonialism.

It was no more than a mask, though, behind which a far deeper change was going on: India was discovering the catch-as-catch-can cosmopolitanism of a city thrown together by purely economic happenstance. The back streets of older, courtly towns — the *mohallahs* of Delhi or the *pols* of Ahmedabad — have the integrity of villages, and also something of their monotony. But in eclectic Bombay, even the byways teem like a bazaar scene as described by Kipling. Castes and sects jostle each other, flog their wares, worship their several gods, tend to their toilettes, haggle, flirt and brawl — all at kerbside. This is an India that few of the British *burra sahibs* ever cared to see. Yet it is the most vital legacy of Empire.

The city came up in the high summer of the Raj, a late bloom compared with the likes of Calcutta or Madras. Always a rich and venal town, Bombay had a dynamism that straightaway translated into an unabashedly materialistic building boom in the late 19th and early 20th centuries, when cotton fortunes flourished. Then the city's physical form was frozen in this state by quixotic post-Independence property laws that failed utterly in their declared intention of bridling undue concentration of wealth, but effectively stymied urban renewal.

The result is what looks, superficially, like a northern English city of the 1930s, little changed in architecture or plan, but left to steam on a tropical coast. The sense of time-warp is inescapable as you stand before the monumental bric-a-brac of Flora Fountain and watch the antique motorcars reeling past the portly bank facades.

But appearances are deceptive. The city is not so much embalmed as pickled: preserved in its outward forms, but permeated with flavours quite alien to the British original. And, in the end, it is the Indian *masala* (spice mixture) that keeps the Raj ambience intact. Consider, for instance, the lawns of the Bombay Gymkhana, coaxed into velvety verdure by a team of a half-dozen barefoot coolies dragging a massive roller twice daily. Or the swarms of white-flannelled cricketers that still turn out on the city's *maidans* every Sunday. Or the endowed private libraries where British bookishness melds with an almost Vedantic reverence for old texts to draw a hushed crowd of readers devoutly perusing 1960s vintage back numbers of *Punch* or *Country Life*.

end have been turned over to military use, with Mazgaon to the north emerging as the commercial shipping hub. Traces remain of the erstwhile maritime bustle of the district: the stolid, stone **Port Trust building**, the ornate headquarters of once-proud (and now bankrupt) shipping companies and the greystone **Old Customs House**. Nearby are the **Reserve Bank of India** (the country's central bank) and the **Mint**.

Pride of place along Bhagat Singh Road, though, must go to the colonnaded **Town Hall**, which houses the **Asiatic Society**, by far the grandest of Bombay's endowed libraries. It is not just the somewhat frayed elegance of the building, with its spiral staircases, wrought-iron loggias, carved teak bookcases and marble statuary. Nor is it even the dusty, mouldering and idiosyncratically catalogued collection of 800,000 volumes, including 10,000 manuscripts and such rare first editions as a 14th-century *Divine Comedy* (worth US$3 million). The real charm of the place lies in its congregation of bibliophiles, among both the readers and the 87-member staff. Somebody there will always be ready to share a wealth of information on your subject, particularly if it is related to Indian antiquities. Chronically starved for funds and cramped for space, the Society is still soldiering on into its 187th year.

From the musty recesses of the Asiatic Society, it is a pleasure to come blinking out into the formal floral extravaganza of Elphinstone Circle across the street (now renamed **Horniman Circle**, after an Irish-born newspaper editor who proved a staunch Indian nationalist).

The circle is especially lively during the lunch hour, when the giant central fountain casts a cooling spray. Itinerants in red bandanas have set up impromptu ear-cleaning parlours outside the gardens.

On the far side of the circle, the **St Thomas Cathedral** (named after the doubting apostle) dozes in its vestigial churchyard, unperturbed by the surrounding swirl of Vir Nariman Road, a main shopping street. Inside, marble monuments (many by the same 19th-century sculptors whose work graces St Paul's in London) understate the romance and overstate the idealism of the Raj.

From Vir Nariman Road, the shopping district extends up Dr Dadabhai Naoroji (DN) Road and Pherozeshah Mehta Road. Besides the fusty old department stores (now run by various government agencies and offering bargain handicrafts), these streets offer old family shops purveying everything from vintage cameras to dried fruits.

The arcaded sidewalks are also cluttered to the point of near-impassability with vendors of real or imitation smuggled imports, rotogravured icons, cheap knitwear, snacks and second-hand books. At night, the wares change: 100-rupee prostitutes ply their trade among the arches.

Anchoring the northern end of DN Road looms the extravagant Gothic fantasy of **Victoria Terminus** (VT). With its flying buttresses, allegorical friezes, stained-glass windows and gargoyle-encrusted dome, the depot is as ornate as St Pancras Station in London, which is of similar vintage. But St Pancras never had scores of rural migrant families camped out in its waiting rooms — bedrolls, cooking pots, children, chickens and all. Nor does it host a half million commuters twice daily. Nor can it begin to rival VT's collection of beggars, porters, snack chefs, patent medicine vendors, preachers, fakirs and pickpockets.

From VT, return to Mukharji Chowk via Waudby Road, where merchant grandees' villas vie with each other in rococo pretentiousness. Beyond Flora Fountain, walk along Cross Maidan, sometime home to tent circuses, religious revival camps and even the annual general meetings of corporations. Then follow Mayo Road past the many-gabled **High Court** and the **University**, with its crypto-Venetian loggias embellished with political graffiti. The Gothic clocktower is incongruously ornamented with worthies in oriental garb representing India's various castes and sects.

The new generations of the same castes and sects — in natty knitwear, instead of flowing robes, these days — continue to mingle around the bandstand at Cooperage, near Oval Maidan. The scene of a heterogeneous gaggle of children sharing a playground and pony ring may seem prosaic to outsiders, but for India it is rare — a testimonial to the cosmopolitanism that continues to justify Bombay's Raj-era sobriquet (emblazoned on its seal): 'Urbs primus in Indus'.

West End Walk

Marine Drive, Chowpatty and Malabar Hill are where Bombay goes to preen and admire itself. These places present some of the best views of the city. Also some of the best views of viewers viewing the city — unbeatable for crowd-watching.

From the surf's edge, across the 100-metre- (330-foot-) long beach of Chowpatty, you can see the whole arc of the **Queen's Necklace** (as the ritzy seaside boulevard of **Marine Drive** was nicknamed by its imperialist builders) and the high-rise skyline beyond. From atop **Malabar Hill**, the roofscapes, seascapes and cloudscapes you can see are among Bombay's snazziest. Priciest, too, in terms of real estate values.

But looking is free, as demonstrated daily by the thousands of less affluent Bombayites who come to this part of town to catch a five-star view. Day trippers of all types: shy courting couples, families on picnics, Jain and Hindu ascetics, loafing office workers, sand-sculptors,

Parsis gather outside the imposing doorway of their temple

crank orators, schoolchildren and college kids playing truant, stupefied junkies, *kabadi* teams (see Sports, page 73), yoga clubs, swimmers, shitters, washerwomen, fishwives and the occasional foreign tourist.

This diverse multitude has attracted to **Chowpatty** an equally heterogeneous floating population of professional servitors, moochers or hangers-on: snack and *paan* vendors, masseurs, pony-leaders, dope pushers, pickpockets, beebee-gun shooting galleries, contortionists, snake charmers, monkey-trainers, *hijras* (eunuchs), lepers, balloon men, flower girls and lots more.

In the middle of the beach, unruffled by all the goings-on around, sits a tree-shaded Koli fishing village. At the end of the monsoon, when the swell calms down enough for them to relaunch their boats, they adorn the craft with pennants and flowers and appease the sea with coconut offerings. Another Hindu rite celebrated at Chowpatty is the annual thread-tying ceremony initiating young boys into the Brahmin caste.

Sadhus (world-renouncing Hindu adepts) practise on Chowpatty such austerities as burying themselves head-first in the sand with only their yoga-posturing legs protruding. Also such inausterities as inhaling quantities of hashish (sacred to Lord Shiva), which they have been known to share with passers-by.

Chowpatty is also the scene of the local equivalent of Carnival in Rio, the Ganesh Chaturthi Festival (see page 90). Two-storey-tall idols of Bombay's potbellied, elephant-headed patron god trundle down to the sea, attended by hundreds of thousands of capering devotees. It is a testimonial to Bombay's efficiency and cosmopolitan tolerance that this orgiastic blow out happens year after year without even unduly snarling traffic, let alone sparking riots.

Walking up Harvey Road from the beach, you cannot miss the curious bobbin-shaped cupola atop the **Bharatiya Vidya Bhavan**, headquarters of one of the reformist Hindu revival movements of the early 20th century. The building is an important concert and lecture venue.

There is always some edifying programme going on — elocution contests, anti-dowry *swayamvara* (in which youngsters choose their own mates in defiance of the conventions of Indian matchmaking, in which caste and astrology usually play a part), national integration rallies — and you can usually get into an earnest 'whither India' discussion there. The Bharatiya Vidya Bhavan also has a multi-lingual library on Vedantic studies and a wonderful bookstore for translated Hindu classics.

A couple of blocks further, turn left into shady Laburnum Marg. Mahatma Gandhi used to stay at house number 19, called **Mani Bhavan**, on this street, when he visited Bombay (see page 38). He was arrested here in 1932 and taken off for one of his many prison terms. The building now houses the **Gandhi Museum**, a 20,000-volume research library, a film and recording archive, a photo display and a set of dioramas on the Mahatma's life. A few elder Gandhians, like the Centre's director, Dr Usha Mehta, frequent the place and might be glad to share their first-hand recollections of the independence struggle and its saintly leader.

From Mani Bhavan continue west on Laburnam Marg to the corner, then turn left to rejoin Hughes Road, the main artery. Diagonally across the boulevard is the entrance to **Babulnath Mandir**, easily spotted by the floral riot of the garland-vendors who cluster around the gateway. *Sadhus*, too, camp out at the entrance, drying their saffron robes on the railing and snoozing on the stairs. A few holy cows, their horns beribboned, fatten on florists' refuse and offerings from the devout. The temple itself, reached up a picturesque stone staircase, is less interesting tc look at than the flock of devotees.

Behind Balbunath rises the steep flank of Malabar Hill, laced with well-worn shady paths and bubbling streams (at least during the monsoon). The tangled vegetation, wild orchids, giant butterflies and mossy scent attest to Bombay's jungle antecedents. A few squatters' shanties still nestle amidst this sylvan idyll. By consistently opting for the right-hand fork at every branching of the trail, you will come out at

Ridge Road just below the Parsi **Towers of Silence**. These seven massive, brooding, vine-festooned cairns are where Parsis lay out the naked cadavers of their dead to be picked clean by vultures. Outsiders are barred entry, so it is left to your imagination to embellish the gloomy prospect as viewed from the road – the precipice above, abruptly sheering off into a flat ridge; the crooked trees, just right for roosting talons . . .

Bombay folklore has it that the vultures, perhaps drowsy from their feasting, sometimes let slip choice bits on to the luxury high-rises and public promenades nearby. For whatever reason, the authorities thought it best to roof over the municipal reservoir just south of the Towers of Silence along Ridge Road. The resulting plateau was turned into a formal garden, with trim hedgerows, floral mazes and sculptured bushes.

This **Hanging Garden** (officially named after Sir Pherozeshah Mehta, a turn-of-the-century nationalist barrister) offers stunning views both to the east (over Queen's Necklace) and the west (where sunsets glint in the open Arabian Sea). Mornings, the park fills up with yoga and calisthenics devotees; evenings, with smoochers.

This area is the ritziest in Bombay, where the mansions of old mercantile families are gradually giving way to deluxe apartment blocks for diplomats, multinational executives and 'black money' nouveaux riches. Maharashtra's Chief Minister has his residence here, near the palatial state guest-house. Just down the Ridge Road from the Hanging Gardens is the gaudy 19th-century **Jain Temple**, a testimonial to the wealth of the community that built it. The opulent jewel-box interior contrasts with the white-robed simplicity of the Jain ascetics who stop off there on their pilgrimages.

The **Kamala Nehru Children's Park**, just across Ridge Road from the Hanging Gardens, offers similar views plus a smattering of playground equipment. Visitors need not bother scaling the concrete 'Old Lady's Shoe': it is easy to get stuck in the crush of day-trippers of all ages swarming up and down the claustrophobic two-storey spiral staircase inside.

If you are ready for a rest stop, the gateways of these two parks feature an assortment of kerbside vendors offering soda-pop, ice cream, *bhel puri*, *paan*, *channa* and such (see pages 61–5). Or, for a sit-down snack, try the Naaz Café right next to the Children's Park. The food in this Parsi-run establishment is nothing special and the service is slow, but the views are spectacular. Beer is served on all but the topmost of its three terraces.

A rest stop on Malabar Hill is so venerable a tradition that Lord Rama himself is said to have paused here, a couple of millennia BC, while heading south to Sri Lanka to liberate his wife from the clutches of a demon kidnapper. At the spot where he stopped, he fashioned a hasty *lingam* (phallic totem, see page 99, Elephanta) out of sand to worship Lord Shiva.

That accounts for the name of the place: **Walkeshwar**, or 'Sand Lord'. The purportedly original *lingam* is still worshipped in an architecturally undistinguished temple of recent vintage. Walkeshwar Marg is a southern extension of the Malabar Hill Ridge Road that leads to the Maharashtra Governor's residence, whose Raj splendours may not be visited by the public without special permission. To reach the temple, turn right on Banganga Marg, named after the sacred pool that sprang up where Lord Rama shot an arrow into the earth.

The **Banganga** is gathered in a soccer-field-sized tank at the foot of the temple. The pool is surrounded by step-like ghats and ringed by lesser temples and low-rise tenements, relics of a less urbanized age. In the stones of the ghats are embedded several ancient and beautiful carvings, still garlanded and smeared with vermilion *tikka* by the devotees that come daily for a purifying dip there.

But the sanctity of the waters does not prevent hundreds of people from using them in performing their daily toilettes. Indeed, a fringe of ramshackle, jerry-built slums now rings the tank like some sort of algae. Paper, soap suds and other detritus accumulates at the end of the pool and in the pre-dawn, the sound of Vedic chanting vies with the hawking of hundreds of squatters brushing their teeth. Behind the *lingam* temple, another ad hoc settlement clings to the seaside rocks: an encampment of *dhobis*, or laundrymen.

Overlooking the whole prospect — temple, tank, slums, washlines and embalmed 19th-century village — loom the gimcrack skyscrapers of the rich, barely 20 years old and already going to seed. The serried contrasts aptly sum up the paradoxes, dilemmas and eclectic charm of modern Bombay.

Museums and Galleries

Amidst the snarl of some of Bombay's busiest traffic, the gardens of the **Prince of Wales Museum** (closed on Mondays) present an island of tranquillity. Statuary, ranging from early Chalukyan to pompous Victorian, nestles among the carefully landscaped shrubbery. Gaggles of schoolchildren and busloads of villagers maintain an uncharacteristic hush as they picnic in the gardens, awed, perhaps, by the grey basalt and yellow sandstone edifice built in 1914 by George Wittet, architect of many of Bombay's more imposing public edifices.

The building is just as impressive from the inside, with its sweeping staircases, long galleries and four tiers of loggias around the domed central well. Its long, unobstructed lines of sight ensure that from most vantage points the visitor can glimpse several exhibits at once, conveying an overall impression of rich profusion.

That impression seems to have been enough to satisfy curators for much of the museum's history. Exhibits rarely varied, and the presentation was stolidly conventional: pedestals, glass cases and terse labels. Lately, though, the museum has gone in for more imaginative displays.

The collection of Indus Valley artifacts, while by no means the most comprehensive in India, is especially well turned out. The pieces are thematically linked and introduced with lucid, informative captions and diagrams (in which the Prince of Wales staff were assisted by a German archaeological team).

The collection of Nepali and Tibetan art is also strikingly displayed in a separate gallery whose muted tones bring out the glory of the *thankas* (religious scrolls) and icons. The natural history section, too, features lifelike dioramas that present the bird and animal specimens in replicas of their natural habitats.

The museum's great pride is its collection of over 2,000 miniature paintings. It may not be the largest such collection in India, but it is one of the most complete. Almost all the significant schools of miniature painting are represented by fine examples.

Not until the 14th century did artists in India turn their attention from the rich, millennia-old tradition of wall-painting (dating back to the Ajanta Caves and beyond) to the miniature. The impetus was part technological (improved brushes, papers and pigments); part economic (the rise of a courtier class of potential collectors) and part cultural (the need to disseminate doctrines in an age of religious proselytization).

All three of these factors arose from India's confrontation with the Islamic world. But India made sweeping changes to the Persian prototypes of miniature painting. Drawing on the subcontinent's own indigenous tradition of finely detailed palm-leaf manuscripts, Indian artists wrought their own distinctive styles. Within a decade, the Mughal monopoly on miniatures was challenged by rival schools of painting under the non-Muslim courts of the Rajput and Pahari kingdoms.

The Prince of Wales' miniatures are organized to show the development and diversification of these different schools, according to painting curator Dr Kalpana Desai. Prize exhibits include sets of thematically unified paintings on such subjects as the *amours* of the god Krishna and his bride Radha, the months and seasons, the assorted *ragas* (musical modes), epic poems, saints and ascetics.

ENTERPRISES

Dr Desai makes a point of keeping most of the collection on public display. Building on a core collection donated by 19th-century merchant princes, the museum is still acquiring paintings on the market, as well as by donation from its cultured benefactors.

Collectors of a different kind have been donating their prize specimens for over a century to the Prince of Wales Museum's neighbouring institution, the **Bombay Natural History Society** (BNHS) (closed on Mondays). One whole floor of Hornbill House, the Society's headquarters, is devoted to beetles and butterflies, all neatly

Festivals

Lord Shiva's dance of cosmic destruction and regeneration is commemorated on a moonless night of February or March. Bombay devotees perform pilgrimages to Elephanta Island in the harbour, despite the officially 'deconsecrated' status of the ancient Shivaite cave temples there.

Holi, also sometime between February and March, marks the onset of springtime. After a bout of spring-cleaning, urbanites treat themselves to a day of abandoned mess-making. They douse each other with coloured powder and water (signifying, supposedly, the blooms of spring). Fun to watch but be sure to have on only clothes you are ready to part with. The festival also commemorates the amours of the archetypal lovers of the Hindu pantheon, Krishna and Radha.

Around March or April, Jains celebrate the **birth of** their sage, **Mahavir**, with temple rites. The Goan version of **Carnival**, at about the same time, combines Latin gaiety with Indian pomp.

Dalit ('untouchable') neo-Buddhists celebrate the **birth, enlightenment and elevation to nirvana of the Buddha** all on the same day, which falls sometime in May or June. Best place to witness the observances is at the Buddhist temple in Worli.

During **Raksha Bandhan**, sometime in August–September, girls ceremoniously tie *rakhis* (gaudy amulets) on their brothers and other boys they regard as their protectors.

Pateti, the **Parsi New Year**, also falls at about this time. Festivities can be best observed at the open fire temple near the Central Telegraph Office at Fountain. A fortnight later comes the birth anniversary of the prophet Zarathustra.

Gokulashtami, or Govinda, riotously commemorates the exploits of the baby Krishna, particularly his celebrated filching of his stepmother's cream pot. To symbolically re-create this event, clay pots are strung between upper-storey balconies of Bombay *chawls* (tenements) and filled with sweets, curds, saffron and money. To snare the loot, troops of taxonomized and stashed away in varnished oak cabinets. Another floor contains hundreds of jars full of embalmed reptiles, plus drawer after drawer of bird and animal pelts.

The keepers of these wonders seem to love nothing better than to expound upon their treasures for the benefit of any passing visitor. You can even join the society as a temporary member for the duration of your stay in Bombay. That entitles you to use BNHS' extensive library of nature books, including some wonderful old tomes illustrated with hand-tinted etchings. Lectures and slide shows go on in the

youngsters form human pyramids to reach the pots. Most of the action takes place in the afternoon.

To mark the end of the monsoon (around September), Kolis launch their boats, with bright pennants flying, on **Nariel Purnima**. At about the same time, Brahmins fast and bathe in the sea to renew the sacred thread that denotes their high-caste status.

Bombay Kerelites from Matunga to Borivili celebrate their harvest festival, **Onam**, during the early autumn.

But the biggest blow out of the year must be **Ganesh Chaturthi**, when seemingly half the city turns out in the streets to orgiastically escort the larger-than-lifesize idols of the elephant-headed god Ganesh. This potbellied god of luck and intellect is perhaps the nearest thing to Bombay's patron deity. The immersion of the idols in the sea — especially at Girgaum Chowpatty — draws hundreds of thousands, cutting across caste and creed lines. The observance was originally promoted by freedom-fighters as a way to get around British anti-assembly strictures.

Dussehra, around October, celebrates the victory of Lord Rama over the demon king of Lanka, Ravana. A re-enactment of the *Ramayana*, called Ram Lila, can be seen at Chowpatty and elsewhere in the city. The burning of Ravana on the last day is the high point. South Indians, on the other hand, celebrate their own Ravana Lila in their suburban ghettoes.

Diwali, the Festival of Lights, is celebrated with plenty of fireworks, sweets and family visits. It also marks the beginning of the business year and the onset of the prime wedding season.

The timing of Muslim holidays is set according to the lunar calendar, so it is hard to predict when they are going to fall in terms of solar months. During the lunar month of **Ramadan**, Muslims fast all day and feast all night. The best night-market for outdoor food stalls is along Mohammed Ali Road in Byculla. Flagellant processions of Shiite Muslims commemorate the martyrdom of the Prophet Mohammed's grandson during the ten-day festival of **Muharram**.

Hornbill House auditorium several nights a week.

The society plans bird-watching or botanical outings in the nearby countryside on most weekends. Every couple of months, the BNHS organizes longer trips to one or another of India's remarkable nature preserves. It could be anything from Terai jungles to the Alpine meadows of the Himalaya to undersea coral gardens. Well-versed naturalists lead the tours, although the groups also include a healthy leavening of enthusiastic amateurs.

Another hobbyist group that organizes field trips is the **Bombay Camera Club**. You can contact the secretary by phoning 495-2311. At the society's headquarters above the Central Camera Shop at 195 D N Road, there are even a couple of rather rudimentary darkrooms you can use for black-and-white processing. Contests and studio sessions are held monthly. Photo aficionados now have a gallery of their own, as well, at the National Centre for the Performing Arts, Nariman Point.

Contemporary artists display at such downtown galleries as the **Chetana**, the **Bajaj** and the **Chemould**. Perhaps the most prestigious venue is the **Jehangir Gallery** adjacent to the Prince of Wales Museum. The quality of exhibits varies widely, however. One section of the Jehangir, at least, is always a reliable hit with local culturati: the Samovar coffee terrace that faces onto the museum gardens. This and the Press Club bar on Azad Maidan (near the Times of India building, St Xavier's College and the J J School of Art) are Bombay's nearest equivalent of a Bohemian bistro.

Elephanta Caves

It may not be the oldest of India's sacred caves, nor the grandest, nor the best preserved. But scholars agree that the rock-cut Shiva temple on Elephanta island is one of the most masterly in conception and craftsmanship. It is also by far the most accessible, an easy day trip by harbour launch from downtown Apollo Bunder in front of the Taj Mahal Hotel.

And it offers an ideal antidote to the fast pace and illusory 'Westernism' of the city. Bombayites know this and flock there in droves. They are festive and friendly enough and, anyway, crowds and touts must have been part of the scene at this pilgrimage site since at least the seventh or eighth century.

Escapism is precisely what Elephanta was designed for by some anonymous genius more than a millennium ago: a way out of everyday appearances into a deeper realm of meaning. The temple establishes a world of its own through the compelling geometry of its floorplan, its naturalistic three-dimensional carving style and the subtle play of

The Caves at Elephanta

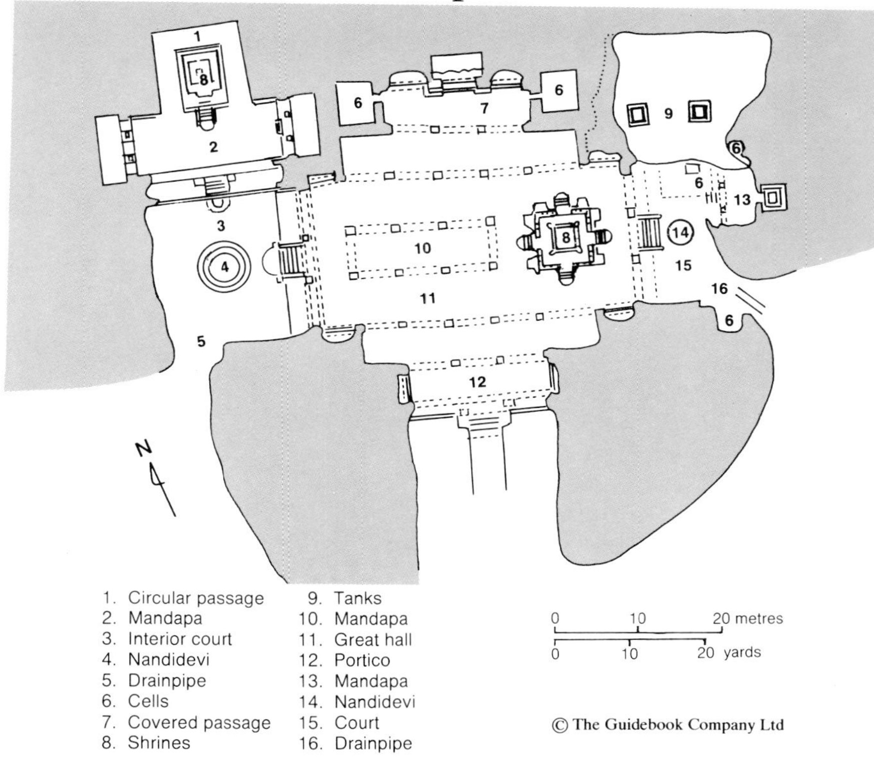

indirect light in its recesses due to the open, colonnaded 'verandas' that surround it on three sides. These features were unprecedented in the rock-cut architecture of the time.

The siting of the temple also enhances the feeling of separation from the mundane. To penetrate its secrets, the visitor has to negotiate three distinct passages: over ten kilometres (six miles) of ocean from Bombay, then up a steep, parched hillside and finally into the 'breathing' shadows of the cave itself.

Considering the psychic distance travelled, the trip is pretty good value for Rs16 per adult by ordinary launch, Rs30 by deluxe (with guide) or Rs40 during the monsoon. Boats depart hourly from dawn through early afternoon.

Magic on a Modest Hillock

The magic begins almost as soon as you leave Apollo Bunder. The harbour offers a grander panorama of Bombay than you will get from anywhere onshore. Away from the city's throb, you can spot the sources of its power: the port, smokestacks and skyscrapers that bespeak its commercial might, the warships and gun batteries that defend it, the tankers and refineries that fuel it, even the sleek-domed atomic reactor at Trombay.

But the most mysterious power of all resides in what looks, from the sea, like no more than a modest hillock. It is only when you reach the island and start hiking up the 100-odd steps which link the jetty with the summit that you appreciate the dimensions of Elephanta.

If you come during the hot months (April–May and again in October), the chances are that you will be grateful for the offerings of the fizzy drink-*wallahs* and the awning shade of the trinket vendors, noisome as they are. Even if you ride a sedan chair to the top (Rs40 subject to haggling), the combined dazzle of the overhead and ocean-reflected sunlight can leave you giddy.

All the more breathtaking, then, to plunge suddenly into the semi-shadow of the cave through an unassuming stone-cut loggia under the beetling, vine-festooned brow of the hill. When your eyes adjust, the first form you can make out is the famed three-headed bust of Shiva, the iconographic centrepiece of the temple.

Its size and distance from where you stand are made ambiguous by the forest of stone columns in the centre of the cave and the indirect illumination that constantly shifts according to the time of day, the season and the weather. The closer you come to the three-headed Shiva, the more this shimmering gloom seems to animate the sculpture. The living rock practically glows.

The left profile presents Shiva the destroyer, festooned with snakes and skulls, who purges the world's impurities. On the right is Shiva the blissful and welcoming celebrant, jewel-bedecked and flower-garlanded. The central head, in full frontal view, shows the abstracted face of the meditative Shiva. Scholars of Hindu symbolism theorize that the image implies two more Shiva heads, one facing south into the bowels of the hill and the other pointed straight up.

Whatever the iconographic merits of this argument, the sculptural style of carving in-the-round at Elephanta strongly suggests that there is more to the figure than meets the eye. Nor is this implicit imagery confined to the colossal bust of Shiva. The same high relief is shown in the other eight didactic panels in the main temple as well. Much more than in other cave shrines of similar vintage, the Elephanta vignettes come off as dioramas, rather than simple flat friezes.

The result is an incomparably rich panoply of emblematic figures and a subtle juxtaposition of symbols and forms, not only within each scene but also among the various panels (see plan, page 95). Thus, the stark serenity of the yogic Shiva offsets the dynamism of the cosmic dancer on the opposite side of the north portal. And the angularity of the demon-slaying panel contrasts with the sheer voluptuousness of the scenes of Shiva with his consort, Parvati.

Shiva–Parvati images dominate the south wall: their marriage, their channelling of the River Ganga upon its descent from heaven, their merger into a single androgynous figure. Two of the panels show domestic scenes of Shiva and Parvati in their abode on the holy Mount Kailash. This peak, scholars believe, is symbolically mirrored not only in the hillock of Elephanta, but also in the 36-square mandala (axially symmetrical cosmic diagram) defined by the cave temple's colonnades.

The mandala has two axes. One runs north to south, past the didactic panels towards the great bust of Shiva, always deeper into the half-light of the cave. The east–west axis, accented by the false ceiling beams, defines the line of religious processionals from the east courtyard — originally the temple's main entrance — to the 'sanctum sanctorum'.

Flanked by guardian deities and silhouetted against the light streaming in from the west veranda, this shrine occupies the 37th square of the mandala. It contains a massive, monolithic phallus, the

The Way of the World

Study these four men washing down the steps of this unpalatable Bombay hotel. The first pours water from a bucket, the second scratches the tiles with a twig broom, the third uses a rag to slop the dirty water down the steps into another bucket, which is held by the fourth. After they have passed, the steps are as dirty as before; but now above the blackened skirting-tiles the walls are freshly and dirtily splashed. The bathrooms and lavatories are foul; the slimy woodwork has rotted away as a result of this daily drenching; the concrete walls are green and black with slime . You cannot complain that the hotel is dirty. No Indian will agree with you. Four sweepers are in daily attendance, and it is enough in India that the sweepers attend. They are not required to clean. *That is a subsidiary part of their function, which is to* be *sweepers, degraded beings, to go through the motions of degradation. They must stoop when they sweep; cleaning the floor of the smart Delhi café, they will squat and move like crabs between the feet of the customers, careful to touch no one, never looking up, never rising. In Jammu City you will see them collecting filth from the streets with their bare hands. This is the degradation the society requires of them, and to this they willingly submit. They are dirt; they wish to appear as dirt.*

Class is a system of rewards. Caste imprisons a man in his function. From this it follows, since there are no rewards, that duties and responsibilities become irrelevant to position. A man is his proclaimed function. There is little subtlety to India. The poor are thin; the rich are fat. The petty Marwari merchant in Calcutta eats quantities of sweets to develop the layers of fat that will proclaim his prosperity. 'You look fat and fresh today' is a compliment in the Punjab. And in every Uttar Pradesh town you might see the rich and very fat man in cool, clean white sitting in a cycle-rickshaw being pedalled by a poor and very thin man, prematurely aged, in rags. Beggars whine. Holy men give up all. Politicians are grave and unsmiling. And the cadet of the Indian Administrative Service, when asked why he has joined the service, replies after some thought, 'It gives me prestige'. His colleagues, who are present, do not disagree. It is an honest reply; it explains why, when the Chinese invade, the administration in Assam will collapse.

V S Naipaul, An Area of Darkness

lingam form in which Shiva is worshipped. The daily presence of fresh cut flowers in the *lingam* chamber suggests the reverence in which Elephanta is still held by Shiva devotees.

The shrine dates back to the time of the Brahminical resurgence after the decline of Buddhism in India. That could place it anywhere from AD 600 to 750. The precise dating is hard to pin down in the absence of any remaining textual evidence. Eighteenth-century European accounts relate that the Portuguese, during their ascendency in Western India, stumbled upon a chiselled inscription in the main temple, but it was somehow lost when they shipped it back to Lisbon in the vain hope of deciphering it.

The inscription was not all the Portuguese destroyed. Iconoclastic missionaries and vandal troopers are blamed for much of the damage to the sculptures. One Portuguese commander reportedly even took to firing his cannon inside the cave because he liked the echo. Muslim rulers, also, bricked in some of the 'heathenish' carved panels, which damaged the sculpture when the mortar was later removed. And the British, for their part, used rubble from some of the lesser ruins as landfill when they built up Bombay.

The latest threat comes from the dynamiting for the newly built auxiliary port of Nava Sheva, just opposite Elephanta on the mainland. Already, hunks of the mountain have collapsed in some of the minor caves on the eastern side of the island, facing the blast sites. A resident crew from the Archaeological Survey of India works year round to control seepage by draining the mountaintop and to shore up the caves with stone-cut columns faithful to the ancient designs. But it is a race against time, as the blasting continues.

Worli and Beyond

For tourists and the gilded rich, Bombay is synonymous with the narrow fringe ringing Backbay. This area contains most of the city's more visible and accessible charms and the greatest concentration of historic sites. It also comprises some of the priciest real estate in the world, far beyond the reach of the average working Bombayite.

So the middle class has expanded instead into the centre and north of the island and the nearby reaches of the mainland. These neighbourhoods may not be much to look at, as viewed through the window of a hurtling taxi en route from the airport. But to their inhabitants, they are self-contained worlds full of amenities.

Here are the liveliest markets, the best little hole-in-the-wall restaurants, the workaday temples, mosques and churches where the city offers its most earnest prayers. These hidden attractions are not easy to find, though, without the help of local contacts.

Luckily, the 'City Diary' column of the daily newspaper can help you make the contacts you need. Film societies, music circles, discussion groups and hobbyist associations of every stripe enliven suburban life. Outsiders are usually welcome to their listed activities, and acquaintances made there can offer entrée to the community. There is no telling what these serendipitous encounters may yield. It is best to approach the suburbs without preconceptions or precise agendas. Still, some broad brush neighbourhood sketches may help you get around:

Mahalaxmi Racecourse is named, somewhat optimistically, after the Hindu goddess of wealth. In the pre-dawn, hundreds of Bombayites turn out here for their morning constitutionals. The high-rise corncob of the cylindrical **Nehru Centre** looms north of Mahalaxmi. Here is the planetarium, a convention centre, a concert-cum-movie auditorium and a children's science centre.

The local **Amateur Riders' Club** offers polo and hurdle-jumping, as well as basic riding classes. During the winter racing season (November–April) thoroughbreds converge here from all over India. **Gallops Restaurant** serves an English breakfast on the racecourse lawns amidst the bustle of morning training. The more important races — especially Derby Day — are glittering social events.

Across the road from the racecourse, **Haji Ali Mausoleum** cuts an impressive silhouette against the backdrop of the open sea. The actual building is something of a disappointment from close up, but the approach is dramatic along a narrow causeway that is submerged at high tide. An assortment of beggars line the path. The snack stalls at the end of the causeway are justly celebrated for their fruit juices, sandwiches and milk shakes.

Just beyond the trim lawns of the posh **Willingdon Sports Club** rise the smokestacks of the **Parel textile mills**, the bedrock of many Bombay industrial fortunes. Times have changed, though: most of the mills, perennially on the verge of bankruptcy, are now nationalized to preserve the jobs they provide. A mill tour (arranged through the National Textile Corporation at Apollo Mills) presents a Dickensian vignette of sweat-glistening hordes toiling at clattering antique power-looms.

Further east, the huddled *chawls* (tenements) of Parel give way to the stolid, bourgeois warren of **Byculla**. The neighbourhood still features such institutions as the Chinese cemetery and clan houses, half a dozen synagogues and the faded Anglo-Indian grandeur of the Heritage Hotel, even though emigration has greatly reduced the ranks of the communities that once made for Byculla's ethnic diversity.

The **Victoria and Albert Museum** here features exhibits on Bombay history. The surrounding **Botanic Garden** posts at the entrance a chalkboard 'menu' of what is currently in bloom. In the adjacent **Zoo**, kids can ride ponies, camels and elephants. The V & A's most celebrated pachyderm, however, is the stone one moved there by the British in 1865 from Elephanta island (which took its name from this statue).

The **docklands** of Bombay, east of Byculla, are as tough as their counterparts in other seaports. They are relieved, though, by a couple of anachronistic enclaves: lateen-rigged dhow-style sailing vessels still call at **Haji Bunder** and **Hay Bunder** (near the Tata Oil Mills) from as far away as the Arabian Gulf. Nearby, the neighbourhood of **Mathapakardy** retains its Portuguese village character, complete with tree-shaded lanes, street-side shrines, latticed balconies and tiny tavernas.

The **Goa Ferry Wharf** near here will come back to life when the temporarily suspended overnight packet boat service is restored (sometime in 1990, officials predict). Meanwhile, you can catch cross-harbour 'bumboats' for nearby coastal villages from the **New Ferry Wharf** near Mazgaon (at the end of the number 50 bus line from Victoria Terminus). Boats sail every half hour from 6 am to 5.30 pm. The harbour crossing takes upwards of two hours. For weekends, buy your tickets in advance. The Rewas-via-Manvad ferry calls at villages within trishaw distance of good **swimming beaches**.

A grim no-man's land of tenements and factories separates the docks from the transport hub of **Dadar's rail** and **bus stations**. Amidst this squalor and grime rise the many spires of the rococo **Swami Narayan Temple**. Kerbside stalls in the station area sell cheap dry goods through the week except Monday, when the area turns into a giant **patent medicine bazaar,** full of herbalists, bone-setters, bear-leaders and snake-charmers, with nostrums for all ills.

Beyond the rail hub, in the middle-class residential side of Dadar, lies the heartland of Marathi gentility. The main temple, the **Siddhi Vinayak Mandir**, is an important shrine of Maharashtra's patron deity, the elephant-headed god Ganesh — here depicted with a rightward-twisting trunk, which denotes an especially efficacious, but temperamental, idol. Devotees throng most thickly on Tuesdays.

In Bombay's vernacular-language **theatre district,** productions range from bawdy vaudeville to introspective psychodramas to period-costumed historical plays. Bring a Marathi-language translator to help you get through the playbills at the Chhabildas theatre or the Rabindra Natya Mandir. Also to get through the after-theatre supper menu at the Sindhudurg, where the *thalis* are non-vegetarian with a heavy accent on seafood.

The fishy accent becomes, if anything, even more pronounced further to the north. By the time you reach **Mahim**, you can already catch a whiff of Bombay duck, the local dried fish speciality, mingling with the sometimes rather 'gamey' fragrance of the creek that separates Bombay island from the Indian mainland. Mahim is a Muslim enclave that specializes in making and repairing fine wooden furniture.

On the **Bandra** side of the creek, in the village of **Chimbai**, you can catch more than a whiff of Bombay duck; rather a knock-out stench. Drying fish festoon the balustrades of the Iberian-style houses and Konkani is still the lingua franca. Chimbai is one vestige of Bandra's Catholic past. Others include some grand **churches** (including the miracle-working Mount Mary's) and a few surviving colonial villas surrounded by gardens.

Bandra was the Jesuit bastion during the early days of Bombay's early European occupation (see pages 27–30). But it owes its main religious festival, the week-long **Saint Mary's Fair** (held annually starting 8 September), to a vow made by a 19th-century Parsi worthy. After losing several infant daughters, Jamshedjee Jeejeebhoy pledged to build a causeway linking Bandra with Bombay if his daughter Phirozebai survived beyond the age of seven.

At the fair commemorating fulfilment of his vow, Bombayites of all faiths throng Mount Mary's to offer wax candles moulded according to their particular prayers: baby-shaped candles for those desiring offspring, various parts of the anatomy for those seeking relief from illness, assorted consumer durables or houses for those seeking material betterment.

Materialism is the keynote of the new, high-rise Bandra that has sprung up since Independence. Bombay yuppies rub shoulders with Hindi movie stars in the glitzy boutiques and restaurants that crowd the main boulevards. **Daavat** on Hill Road and **Croissants Etcetera** on Turner Road are the current favourites among upmarket eateries.

For downmarket gourmets, too, Bandra offers some of the best 'dives' in Bombay, including **Saayba's**, a Konkan seafood joint on S V Road, and the vegetarian **New Aram Kaachi Hotel** at the end of the Mahim Causeway. Roadside **foodstalls** near the 'lovers' lane' of **Carter Road** also serve a variety of snacks.

Bird-watchers will soon be able to enjoy a planned **bird sanctuary** in East Bandra. Bikini-watchers congregate at the poolside of the Searock Hotel or the Otters Club in West Bandra. But the biggest concentration of five-star **swimming pools** in suburban Bombay is along the strand in **Juhu**, where international chains and Indian hoteliers have built a row of hostelries to suit every taste and budget.

These hotels cater not only to passengers from the nearby airports, but even to Bombayites seeking a quick getaway from the city's crush. There are miles of sandy beaches to walk on, though not exactly in solitude: the **Juhu strand** is as much of a honky-tonk as Girgaum Chowpatty, but on a grander scale and even more crowded on weekends. Even this far north, the water is too polluted for swimming. For that, the nearest **beaches** are **Madh** or **Marve** (both a rickshaw ride away from Malad station on the Central Railroad). Or — marginally cleaner, still — **Manori**, a ferry ride away from Marve.

Juhu even boasts a sort of spiritual theme-park built by the **International Society for Krishna Consciousness (ISKON)**. Tonsured, saffron-robed Western devotees officiate in the gleaming marble temple with its brightly daubed images. Spiritual seekers from abroad also flock to the **Ananda Marga Ashram** at **Ganeshpuram**, 55 kilometres (34 miles) north of Bombay, despite recent factional feuds within the sect. A nearby **hot-spring** offers mineral baths.

By the time you have gone this far, you are already on the open road leading north to Gujarat. Truckers — and not a few jaded urbanites — drive out here to sample the gourmet delights of the **roadside *dhabas*** that serve premium Punjabi meals alfresco at a fraction of what such fare would cost downtown. As an added bonus, you can follow your feast with a siesta on one of the *charpai* rope cots set out for the road-weary lorry drivers.

One of the first turn-offs on the Ahmedabad trunk road is signposted for 'Vasai', the latter-day spelling of **Bassein**. This was the Court of the North that administered the Portuguese enclaves dotting the coast above Goa. All that is left of this past grandeur are the ancient city walls, with their ornate gates, plus several romantically decomposed churches.

Far older ruins dot the **Krishnagiri Upavan National Park**, reachable by rickshaw from the Borivili station. The Buddhist **Kanheri Caves** here date from the second to the ninth centuries AD. Of the 109 caves, though, only a few are architecturally or sculpturally noteworthy. The best is Cave 3, a galleried *chaitya* congregational hall (see page 158).

For non-antiquarians, the park even has a Lion Safari ride, although the animals tend to be somewhat reticent. The hilltops in the park and the nearby **Aarey Milk Colony** (a model dairy) offer stunning island views. During the monsoon, the greenery is spectacular, complete with tumbling waterfalls.

This verdure has served as a backdrop for many a Hindi movie shot in the backlots of the nearby **film studios**. Others are shot on elaborate indoor sets. Despite the declining fortunes of the Bombay film industry, most of the studios usually have several projects shooting simultaneously. Lunch hours at the studio canteens present an odd assortment of incongruously costumed extras.

Goa

Golden Beaches and Colonial Monuments

A sense of the past can add lustre to the landscapes and resonance to the personalities you meet in Goa. Even by the hoary standards of India, Goan history is especially lengthy and romantic, crammed with clangourous battles, colourful characters and intriguing riddles. Pirates and pilgrims, slavers and saints — all have left their mark.

Today's sleepy villages once served successive Hindu, Arab and Portuguese rulers as the hubs of world-spanning empires. Hermitage caves of Jain and Buddhist ascetics are barely an hour's drive from the rubble of the Portuguese inquisitors' sinister black castle. As an Axis enclave in British India, Goa saw its share of World War II spying. Scuttled Nazi merchant ships still lie at the bottom of Panaji harbour. Some of the stranded German crewmen stayed on, marrying locally.

Early Settlers

There is nothing new in that: beguiling Goa has ensnared sojourners since the Early Stone Age. The first inhabitants seem to have migrated to the coastal plain over the highlands of the Western Ghats, leaving a trail of palaeolithic axes and cleavers along the route of the present-day rail line. Successive overland migrations came also along the coast, first from the south and later from the north.

Just who these early immigrants were is still a subject of scholarly wrangles. Judging from the totemic cults that still persist in Goa and the distinctive ethnology of such surviving 'aboriginal' people as the Kunbis, the original settlers may have been tribes from the Deccan to the north, Malabar to the south, or even as far away northeast as the Brahmaputra valley in Assam. Or they may have been Dravidians displaced by the Aryan advance from Central Asia.

The Aryans themselves seem to have found their way into Goa in early times in the form of the Gaud–Saraswats, a band of Brahmins who cut themselves off from their caste when they compromised their vegetarian scruples by eating fish to tide over a 12-year famine. Other Aryan incursions may have been by sea after the decline of the *Mahabharata*-era city states of Saurashtra in Gujarat.

Sea venturers came from farther afield, too. For a ship setting out from the mouth of the Red Sea and then drifting along the prevailing currents, the most natural Indian landfall would be Goa. As early as 2000 BC, Sumerians knew it as a trading station called Gubi. Phoenicians, Persians and Arabs ventured there as well.

These successive layers of immigrant tribes and cults hardened into a caste hierarchy that has proved resistant to all subsequent religious

MAHARASHTRA
KARNATAKA
Tiracol Fort
River Tiracol
Pernem
Alorna Fort
PERNEM
Harmal Beach
River Chapora
Chapora Fort
Vagator Beach
Anjuna Beach
Mapusa
BARDES
Dicholi
BICHOLIM
SATAR
Carambolim
Sanquelim
Baga Beach
Kalangut Beach
Kalangut
Arvalem Falls
Valpoi
Kandoli
Kandoli Beach
River Goa
Cumbarjua
Old Goa
Raij
Aguada Fort
Magus Fort
Panaji
Basilica de Bom Jesus
Gaspar Dias Beach
Mandovi River
TISWAD
Dona Paula
Dona Paula Beach
Pillar
Tambdi
BONDALA SANCTUARY
To Dharwad
PONDA
River Zuari
Vasco Da Gama
Ponda
Molen
Dubolim
MARMAGAO
BHAGWAN MAHAVEER SANCTUARY
Bogmalo Beach
Velsao Beach
Cansaulim Beach

Goa
Arabian Sea
Colva Beach
Benaulim Beach
Betul Beach
Cape Rama
Agonda Beach
Palolen Beach
River Sal
Rachol Seminary
SALSETE
Margao
Chandor
Sanvordem
SANGUEM
Dudh Sagar Waterfall
Shri Chandreshwar Bhutnath Temple
Quepem
Sanguem
Shri Ramadar Temple
Bally
QUEPEM
Gaundongrem
Shri Mallikarjun Temple
Chauri
CANACONA
COTIGAO SANCTUARY
To Karwar
N
0 2 4 6 8 km
0 2 4 60 miles

and cultural overlays. Even in Catholic churches today, Brahmin and Shudra Christians rarely sit together, much less intermarry. But a more humane legacy is also traceable to Goa's early history — the millennia-old system of primitive communalism that survived as the basis of village organization right up to the end of Portuguese rule.

Village Communes

Each village, or *gaum*, was a self-contained unit of farmers and artisans. Every villager contributed to the commonweal according to his hereditary role. Property was communally held and allotted by the council of elders, which met weekly. All council decisions were unanimous since each member wielded absolute veto power. Services and public works were paid for out of the community fund.

Historians theorize that such a system could have evolved in the tightly knit pioneer communities of prehistoric times. The trim and landscaped hamlets of Goa today, so full of amenities compared with the rest of India's villages, attest to the stewardship of the village councils, or *communidades* as they were called in Portuguese.

After the merger of Goa into the India Union in 1961, however, the newly ascendant politicians dismissed the *communidades* as a hoax designed to perpetuate the 'elders' as a hereditary landed class under the guise of communal ownership. Land reforms parcelled out *gaum* property among residents.

Whatever the merits of the *communidades* and the land reforms, statistics show that Goa's agricultural self-sufficiency has declined over the past 30 years, while migration — both of Goans leaving the state and outsiders coming in — has gathered momentum. And once-communal Goan lands in the vicinity of prime tourist spots or booming cities have become some of India's most hotly traded real estate.

Not that either urbanity or the 'hospitality industry' are exactly new to Goans. Nearly 2,000 years ago Divar Island was already renowned as a pilgrimage site, while Arvalem was a centre of Buddhist monasticism. By the second century, the riverside port of Chandor was already important enough to rate a mention by the Greek geographer Ptolemy. With the decline of Mauryan rule in India (third century BC), Chandor became the capital of local Bhoja rulers. Sixth-century Goan seafarers ranged as far as Bali and Sumatra, where some place names still commemorate the Bhojas.

The Kadambas

Chandor was to change hands repeatedly among such dynasties as the Mauryans, Chalukyas and Siliharas. For all these dynasties, though, Goa was only a sideshow to their main power-plays in the Konkan and the Deccan. It was not until the tenth century, with the rise of the Kadambas, that Goa regained centre-stage status. Even then it was largely by default: only after their ejection from their original stronghold in Mysore did the Kadambas shift their focus to the seaward side of the Ghats.

The Kadambas were of impeccable pedigree, claiming descent from a three-eyed, four-armed demiurge who had sprung up from the ground where Lord Shiva had let fall a drop of sweat during one of his cosmic exertions. More to the point, the Kadambas specialized in breeding exquisite princesses and allying themselves through marriage to neighbouring royalty. But their fortunes had been in eclipse for nearly three centuries prior to their Goan adventure.

After consolidating his hold over Chandor, the founding Goan Kadamba dynast set out with a hundred-ship armada on a thanksgiving pilgrimage to Somnath in Gujarat. He had got no farther than the mouth of the Zuari River, however, when his entire fleet was swamped by a sudden storm — something to visualize on your modern-day Cortalim–Agassaim ferry trip to liven up the otherwise sleepy boat-ride.

The disaster proved fortunate in its way, since the Kadambas were rescued by the colony of Arab traders from the riverside settlement of Hanjaman-nagar. The alliance thus forged helped establish the Kadamba kingdom as the pre-eminent maritime power of its day. The Arabs used Kadamba patronage to make Goa the hub of their far-flung commercial network embracing 14 ports from Bahrain to Java. The kingdom prospered enough for the Kadambas to build a navy that was unbeatable in its time.

By the time of the third dynast, the Kadambas had outgrown their riverine capital of Chandor and annexed the seaside port of Govapuri, from which the name 'Goa' is derived. They built here a splendid city of broad boulevards and plazas, palaces and temples.

Goa Vellem

Today, the Zuari has silted so far upstream that the docks of Goa Vellem (as the place is now called) stand high and dry and overgrown. Palm plantations cover the rubble, although road courses are still discernible. Farmers here routinely turn up ancient carved stones. They are often incorporated into the gingerbread style of architecture of local mansions, while a trove of excavated memorabilia can be viewed in the museum of the nearby Pilar Monastery. But only the massive tank of the goddess Chamunda's temple survives *in situ* to give an idea of the scale of the Kadamba capital.

The apex of Kadamba power was achieved under the reign (1052–

80) of Jayakeshi I, who had himself proclaimed 'Lord of the Konkan and Emperor of the Western Seas'. After his death (by self-immolation, according to legend, due to his inconsolable grief over the death of his pet parrot), the Kadamba rulers found themselves increasingly preoccupied with trying to avoid vassalage to either the Chalyukans or the Hosyalas, who were fighting it out for overlordship of the Deccan. Eventually, by the 13th century, they fell prey to an upstart warlord house, the Yadavas of Devgiri, and Goa reverted to marginal status in the polity of the times.

Muslim Invasions

So it was a trade-rich and relatively defenceless Goa that faced the depredations of the Tughluqs, the first Muslim invaders of the Konkan, around the start of the 14th century. With the break-up of the Tughluq kingdom, Goa fell to one of its offshoots, the Bahmani sultanate, which was locked in a drawn-out combat with the Hindu Vijayanagar empire. Anti-Hindu pogroms got so bad that the tutelary deity of the Kadambas, Saptakoteshwar, had to be plucked out of his temple on the island of Divar and buried in a rice field.

It did not stay there long, though. Saptakoteshwar was unearthed and restored to his temple by a Goan Saraswat insurgent, Madhav Mantri. At the head of a Vijayanagar army, he reclaimed much of the Konkan and ruled, as viceroy, a Goa several times bigger than the modern-day state. For most of the 15th century, Goa remained a Vijayanagar outpost, squarely on the line of confrontation with the Bahmanis.

Goa's Muslims — mostly Arabs and local converts engaged in the horse trade — chose to abandon Hindu-dominated Govapuri (whose harbour was already silted, anyway) in favour of the Mandovi River port of Ella. But Govapuri still remained the base for a Vijayanagar 'navy', under the 'admiralty' of a Kadamba heir, which occupied itself mainly with piratical depredations upon Haj pilgrims.

This practice so affronted the pious and scholarly Bahmani vizier, Khwaja Mahmud Gawan, that he finally extirpated the Vijayanagar coastal enclave after a two-year siege of Goa's seaside forts. Gawan lost no time in razing Goa's Hindu temples. Devotees either buried their gods once again or carried them along on their inland exodus to the highlands around Ponda. These hills remain Goa's Hindu heartland to this day.

Gawan's enemies at the Bahmani court got the sultan to order his assassination on the basis of forged incriminatory letters. Deprived of its able vizier, the sultanate promptly disintegrated. Goa fell to the share of Yusuf Adil Shah, a Persian princeling who had been sold into slavery as a result of court intrigue, bought in Ormuz by Gawan and adopted by him as a son.

Although headquartered in the Deccan fastness of Bijapur, Adil Shah was sufficiently taken with Goa to consider moving his capital to Ella, the Muslim enclave established in Vijayanagar times. The city he laid out there — with its palaces, artisans' quarters, shipyards and riverfront docks — turned out to be the template for the 'Golden Goa' of his Portuguese successors. Even the building that now houses the state secretariat in Panaji was originally built as a beach villa for Adil Shah.

Enter the Portuguese

After Adil Shah's death, his successors began to lose their grip on the outposts of their demesne. So it proved no challenge for the Portuguese expeditionary, Afonso de Albuquerque, guided by a Vijayanagar scout, to take the city in March 1510 with a fleet of 23 ships and 1,200 troops. Two months later, however, the Portuguese 'Commander of the Indian Ocean' had to vacate the city (with as much loot and as many harem beauties as could be conveniently carried) before Adil Shah's avenging troops from Bijapur.

Albuquerque waited in the harbour mouth for reinforcements and, by year end, finally clawed his way back to Ella (or Goa City, as he had re-christened it), rather more strenuously than before. Two Old

St Francis Xavier

One of Goa's most celebrated 16th-century denizens was St Francis Xavier, a co-founder of the Jesuit monastic order (together with his Sorbonne-college friend and fellow Spanish nobleman, St Ignatius of Loyola). In fact, Xavier spent only a few months in Goa, mostly engaged in what would nowadays be described as social work, before launching out on major missionary expeditions in Kerala, Malacca, the Spice Islands and Japan.

Actually, it was as a corpse that St Francis was to make his greatest impact on Goa. Months after his death and burial on an island off the coast of Canton, his body was disinterred and found to be remarkably intact. Shipped back to Goa, Xavier's remains attracted thousands of pilgrims. One lady was stirred to such a frenzy of devotion that she bit off a toe of the corpse. The Vatican, too, required a piece of Xavier: the pope ordered the miraculously preserved right arm to be shipped to Rome as evidence in Xavier's canonization proceedings.

In 1622, shortly after the canonization, the saint's relics were moved to the just completed Basilica de Bom Jesus. The body is now preserved under glass on a raised pediment, perhaps to discourage latter-day souvenir hunters.

Impressive as the basilica may be, the Jesuits left even prouder monuments in Goa, in keeping with the scholarly traditions of their order. Their schools and seminaries set a standard to be emulated by others in the fierce inter-monastic rivalries of the day. A Jesuit rendered the Bible into a classic Konkani translation. Another even trained as a Hindu Brahmin and propounded syncretic rites.

Goa churches commemorate the battle: the well-preserved Our Lady of the Rosary and the eerily overgrown Our Lady of the Mount.

What the plaques and frescos do not recount, however, is the general massacre of Muslim citizens that was ordered once the city was recaptured. Albuquerque saw himself as a crusader in the mediaeval tradition (no wonder, considering how recently the last Moorish enclaves had been expunged from Iberia). His professed mission in Asia was to destroy Islam and expand Christendom.

But that did not keep him from pursuing Portugal's maritime trading advantage at the same time. The year after he established himself in Goa, he set out to forge more links in the chain of Portuguese dominion — Malacca and the Spice Islands.

He was on his way to establishing a bastion at Ormuz when he took ill and turned back to India, only to find on arrival there that he had fallen from favour in Lisbon and his bitterest rival was now installed as governor of Goa.

He was so ill by the time he sailed up the Mandovi, that he had to be carried to the deck in a chair for a last glimpse of his Dourada (Golden City). He died before the ship could dock at Goa. By ranging so far from the Mandovi's shores, Albuquerque left Goa a richer legacy than any he could have achieved had he stayed put: a widely cast eastern empire for which the Golden City served as entrepôt. By the late 16th century, nearly 300 ships a year plied between Goa and Portugal carrying spices, perfumes, gems and gold. The shoals of Goa's coast are to this day littered with promising wrecks, according to the marine archaeology department of India's National Institute of Oceanography in Dona Paula.

Profits from this entrepôt trade quickly created a boom town that rivalled Lisbon itself in ostentation. The hieratic hulks of Old Goa's churches, incongruously looming nowadays out of an unpeopled meadow on the riverbank, attest to the baroque grandiosity of the Portuguese colonials' self-importance. No trace remains of the dense tangle of lanes that once enmeshed these monuments. Nor of the throbbing street-life, crowded with fishwives, *fidalgos*, freebooters and slaves, cutpurses, clerics and opulent courtesans, as described by contemporary diarists. The city boasted the oldest and best hospital in Asia. It also required three jails.

The Inquisition in Goa

Tolerance marked few of the missionaries who went to Goa in the Portuguese wake. Most of them favoured forced conversions, mass baptisms and the razing of Hindu temples. The idol of Saptakoteshwar, the Kadambas' tutelary deity, spent a few years embedded in the masonry of a well, turned on its side to serve as a 'pulley' for the drawstring. Finally it was spirited out of Portuguese territory and enshrined in a remote valley temple in Bicholim (where it can still be seen).

Laws made even the private practice of Hindu rites punishable by confiscation of property. Half the booty thus robbed was to be shared with the 'Christian convert' informers who turned in the covert worshippers. Converts were also the only Goans eligible for government office, and hence for a share in the rich bribes and rake-offs that lubricated the entire apparatus of the colonial entrepôt.

These ungentle methods of batch-processing converts were perfected when the area under Portuguese control abruptly expanded far beyond the original enclave of riverine islands with the annexation of Bardez and Salsete, the last and biggest acquisitions of the 16th-century Velhas Conquistas (Old Conquests). These territories were never actually

Portuguese Rule in Decline

Portuguese power in the world began to wane towards the end of the 16th century, when a botched and pointless Morocco campaign so decimated the Portuguese nobility that the country fell under the sway of the Spanish crown. By the time sovereignty was regained in 1640, Lisbon's moment of maritime glory had slipped past. Upstart imperial challengers — the British and Dutch — carved out Far Eastern empires of their own, usurping Goa's pre-eminence as Europe's entrepôt in Asia. The calibre of Lisbon's men in Goa also deteriorated. From a band of vigorous (if somewhat piratical) adventurers, the Goa administration deteriorated into a bloated bureaucracy with more perks than vision.

Meanwhile, the Indian scene around them had drastically altered. The Vijayanagar and Adilshahi factions, whose rivalries the Portuguese had so long exploited, had finally withered away. In their place, the Konkan and Deccan were to be galvanized by the newly militant Maratha power under the guerrilla general, Shivaji. In 1668, he ousted the feudal lords of Bicholim and Pernem and parked himself for a few weeks in the temple of Saptakoteshwar, on what was then the border of Portuguese Goa. But before he could mount an assault on the European enclave, he had to rush back to defend his own capital

conquered but, rather, wangled out of the Bijapur sultans and their Konkan governors in exchange for promises (later defaulted on) of Portuguese support in their factional wars. Bardez was apportioned to the Franciscans and Salsete to the Jesuits as mission fields.

After the first half century of Portuguese rule in Goa, the net result of all this breakneck Christianization was a legion of nominal converts. But that was not enough for the clerics of Goa (who numbered one to every five Christian citizens of the city and enjoyed powerful influence in Lisbon and Rome). The priests wanted a tighter hold over the life of the colony. So they brought in the Holy Inquisition as a kind of 'thought police'. 'Heretics' were burned in showy, carnival autos-da-fe (acts of faith).

But the real impact of the Inquisition derived less from these public extravaganzas than from the whispered rumours of what went on behind the walls of the Black Palace inherited from Yusuf Adil Shah, where the Dominican interrogators ensconced themselves. Their shadowy reign lasted for over 200 years. When the colony's capital was finally shifted to Panjim (now officially called Panaji), and when in 1830 the Black Palace was razed to provide building stone, piles of human bones were found stashed in its subterranean stairwells.

The Silver Screen

The wet sari, as seen clinging to film actresses, has in recent years come to represent an erotic ideal. In hundreds of films the director contrives ways of leading both the heroine and the bad girl to water. They fall in rivers and the sea. They get caught in the rain and sprayed by gardeners' hoses. They have large liquid eyes, bruised roses for mouths, slightly sulky, and there they stand with their garments clinging. The cinema in India is a sexual frontier, gradually encroaching on conservatism, and is partly devoted to stimulating and gratifying fantasies in a sexually unpermissive society. The giant film hoardings are remarkable, an industry and art form of their own, a colourful part of the city street scene, promising hours of thrusting bosoms, wet saris and gunfire for a few rupees. In blasé Bombay, and Delhi, Calcutta and Madras, the strictly limited eroticism of the cinema has become accepted, although there are always newspaper controversies over films that have supposedly gone too far. But in the villages many find them too strong, and men forbid women to go to the travelling cinemas.

A kiss is rarely seen in an Indian film, being too daring, and too offensive, in a society where such physical pleasures are enjoyed in private. Few Indian couples show affection in public. You hardly ever see boys and girls holding hands, and you never see canoodling in the parks. Indeed, in parks you are more likely to see groups of boys and girls sitting in sexually segregated circles, some yards apart. Thus the question of 'to kiss or not to kiss' in films is a favourite and titillating subject in magazines and newspapers.

Indian girls are modest and many actresses would not only refuse to kiss in a film but would be outraged if asked to do a nude scene. Even partial nudity is rare. The camera usually stops short at a bare back or a generous thigh. Western films are heavily cut. Bosoms heave, but are not bared.

Trevor Fishlock, India File

against Muslim attack.

Shivaji's son, 25 years later, actually went so far as to capture Bardez and Salsete. All the Portuguese viceroy could think of doing was to drag out the relic of Francis Xavier and prayerfully convey the baton of military command into the saint's one remaining hand (see page 113). This seemed to work: the very next day the Marathas lifted their siege and dashed off to combat a sudden attack on their rear by the Mughal emperor Aurangzeb. The Mughal distraction, it turned out, gave Goa nearly a half-century of peace from the Marathas.

In fact, the Marathas indirectly aided the Portuguese in annexing their next territories: Ponda, Quepem, Sanguem and Cancona. The raja of the area, harried by troops of the Mysore adventurer Hyder Ali, sought Portuguese help in exchange for territory. Hyder's vengeful attacks on the Goan coast were scotched when the Marathas and British ganged up on him back in the Deccan, and Ponda remained in the Portuguese fold. Sawantwadi, a petty fiefdom to Goa's north, also made the mistake of inviting in the Portuguese to fend off rivals. The territories of Bicholim, Satari and Pernem had already been occupied, the size of the Portuguese enclave trebled and the present-day boundaries of Goa established by the time the misguided raja realized that he had been double-crossed.

Portugal's allies against the Sawantwadi raja in 1788 had been the fiery Rane clans of Satara. But throughout the following century, these same Ranes were to revolt periodically against Lisbon's viceroys, too, over such issues as taxes and military conscription. This derring-do earned the Ranes a Robin Hood reputation at the time and an *ex post facto* cachet as Freedom Fighters since the merger of Goa into the Indian Union (the present Chief Minister of the State is a Rané).

Resistance to Portuguese Rule

As much as to the martial prowess of the Ranes, though, these revolts owe their impact to the deteriorating strength of the Portuguese. By the turn of the 19th century, the city of Old Goa had to be abandoned. Its port had silted and its population had been decimated by successive epidemics. A new capital, far less grand, was established in Panjim (now Panaji). Britain was already firmly in control of India, and Portuguese mercantile fortunes had so declined that the Goa administration was no longer even self-supporting.

In the early decades of the current century, iron ore mining in north and east Goa emerged as the new mainstay of the economy. Migrant mineworkers tipped the colony's demographic balance from a Catholic to a Hindu majority. New Hindu fortunes were built on ore sales to Japan and the smuggling of all kinds of imports into India.

Goan Catholics, once beneficiaries of the thriving entrepôt trade, were now reduced to exporting manpower: aristocratic Goan families cut a swathe in the arts and professions of India, while more plebeian Goans worked as clerks, cooks, mechanics, musicians and seamen.

Throughout these economic upheavals, Lisbon still hung on to its colonial enclave out of sheer force of habit (and, perhaps, a tinge of reverence for St Francis Xavier). Then, too, the motherland was preoccupied with its own political upheavals: overthrow of the monarchy, a sequence of parliaments and a short-lived republic. In one of these political convulsions, Goa was first promised and then denied a limited autonomy. The Goan protest movement against the 1918 betrayal was led by the crusading journalist and social reformer, Luis de Menezes Bragança, who is still revered as a kind of Goan Nehru.

Menezes Bragança went on courageously protesting colonial injustices even after the establishment of the Salazar dictatorship in Portugal. But Salazar was not one to be moved by liberal appeals to conscience. Nor by non-violent, pro-independence demonstrations by Gandhian *satyagrahis* (adherents of the policy of non-violent resistance). Nor by diplomatic appeals for a negotiated settlement with independent India after the British left the rest of the country in 1947. Finally, Indian Prime Minister Nehru ran out of patience in 1961 and sent in the army.

Once again, the Portuguese viceroy appealed to St Francis Xavier, but this time the ploy failed. Ignoring Salazar's orders to defend the colony to the death (and thereby earning himself eventual condemnation for treason), Governor-General Vassalo de Silva surrendered virtually without a shot.

Getting To, From and Around Goa

Getting There

Entering or leaving Goa from elsewhere in India still has the feeling of crossing an international boundary. Border guards man gateposts on either side of the state line on major approach roads, logging the particulars of all passing vehicles into massive ledgers. Customs officials at Bombay's steamer wharf check disembarking passengers from Goa for smuggled booze. Coming over the ghats from Karnataka, rail passengers have to switch from broad-gauge to metre-gauge carriages.

By Air

Paradoxically, perhaps the smoothest approach to Goa is for those passengers who actually do come directly from outside India on one of the growing number of international flights that land at the state's Dabolim Airport. Foreign airlines are vying for landing rights there to cater to Western package tourists. So far only Lufthansa comes straight to Goa with its Condor flights en route to Kathmandu. But others, including British Airways and Swissair, plan to have Europe-to-Goa routes soon.

As long as international flights to Dabolim are relatively few and largely limited to foreign holiday-makers, the airport is likely to remain the most convenient port of entry into India, free of the overload and the inquisitorial screening of overseas Indian returnees that choke up the international arrival terminals elsewhere in the country. Be sure, though, to avoid the direct Air India flight from Sharjah, which caters to guest-workers from the Gulf — prime targets for the dilatory ministrations of the customs men.

Domestic flights link Dabolim with Cochin and Trivandrum in Kerala, Bangalore and Hyderabad in the Deccan, as well as the main metropolises of Bombay, New Delhi and Madras. Pick-up buses deliver high-rolling tourists to the five-star hotels, but there is no public airport bus, and the taxis at Dabolim like to gouge out fares as high as Rs100 to Panaji. To escape their clutches, catch an airport cab or a yellow-painted taxi-cycle to Vasco, just four kilometres (2.5 miles) away, which is well connected with the rest of Goa by public transport and metered taxis.

By Boat

If you are not pressed for time and your itinerary takes you through Bombay, the steamer link is more leisurely than air travel. Cabin class on the Goa Ferry is luxurious in a faded sort of way, and a bargain (upwards of Rs300 per berth with slight variations, depending upon cabin amenities). But cabin reservations are hard to come by, especially during the peak winter season. If all else fails, try a direct appeal to the passenger services department of the Shipping Corporation of India (SCI, Bombay tel. 2022933, tlx. 011-2371, attention Jagdish Seth, Executive Director, whose brief includes passenger services).

The northbound steamer trip is prettier than the southbound, since the ship plies closer to the coast and calls at the picturesque estuarine ports of the Konkan by daylight, rather than at night. The trip in either direction takes about 24 hours.

Bus and Rail

Quicker and cheaper, albeit less gracious, is the overnight (14-hour) bus ride from Bombay. Night coaches also run between Goa and Bangalore, Mysore or Mangalore (due south on the Karnataka coast). Private bus companies maintain offices on the main plazas of Panaji, Margao and Mapusa. The air-conditioned video coaches, which show Hindi movies during the journey, are costlier and less restful. Shorter bus hauls over the ghats take you to Londa or Hubli, where you can catch trunk-line trains.

The metre-gauge railroad, which goes only to the south side of the Zuari estuary, is no more than a spur line off a spur line: it links up at Miraj with the picturesque, but poky, Maharashtra Express of the Central Railway. Long-distance rail travel times from Goa can be daunting: nearly a full day to Bombay or Bangalore, two days or more to Delhi, Madras, Cochin or Calcutta. Most of these trips entail several train transfers and long stretches without air-conditioned carriages or sleepers — not recommended for any but the most intrepid Indrailpass travellers.

Getting Around

Getting around within Goa can be an adventure. Better not to schedule your day with too much precision, since the timetables of most public conveyances can be rather elastic. Allow even more latitude if your itinerary takes you across the Mandovi River, since the collapse of the Nehru Bridge at Panaji now obliges travellers to queue up for ferries, at least until completion of the new bridge (optimistically scheduled for 1990).

But, despite its uncertainties, travelling around Goa is relatively hassle-free for the relaxed, flexible visitor. There is not much risk of getting stranded in the hinterland or straying too far off the beaten track: English-speaking informants and reasonable pub food are likely

Panaji
N
Mandovi River
Ferry Ramp
Panaji Jetty
Nehru Bridge
Indian Airlines
Police Headquarters and Immigration
Secretariat (Adilshah's Idalcaon Palace)
Avenida Dom Joao Castro
Municipal Market
Heliodoro Salgado Road
Gen Costa Alvares Road
Swamy Vivekanand Rd
Antao de Noronha Rd
Rivara Street
Cunha Road
Ormuz St
Municipal Park
General Post Office
Panaji Church
Pato Bridge
Ribandar Causeway
Dept of Tourism
Gen Bernardo Guedes Road
Afonso de Alburquerque Rd
Dr P Shirgaonkar Rd
Dr Pisurlekar Road
State Bank of India (SBI)
Dr Dada Vaidya Road
Air India
19th June Road
Dr Atmaram Borkar Road
Mahalaxmi Temple
Armada Portuguesa Road
Dr R S Road
Bus Terminal
Museum
Kala Academy
Dr Braganza Pereira Road
Dr Gama Pinto Road
Almirante Reis Road
Ourem Creek
Telephone Exchange
Bishop's House
Ramachandra Naik Rd
Dayanand Bandokhar Marg
St Inez Church
Nanu Tarkar Pednekar Road
Ourem Road
Avenida J Silveira
St Inez Road
© The Guidebook Company Ltd

to crop up in even the remotest villages. **Inter-city buses** are cheap and frequent and packed — often to bursting — with generally friendly and chatty people. **Express buses** run from Panaji to Mapusa in the north and Margao to the south. From these hubs, you can catch local buses to the beaches and villages.

Scores of vehicle **ferries** link the islands that dot the Mandovi estuary, plying at intervals of 10–30 minutes. Ferries also cross the Zuari, Sal, Chapora and Tiracol rivers. Longer-haul launches, like those from Dona Paula to Vasco or up the Mandovi to Bicholim, depart only once or twice a day; check with the main ferry wharf in Panaji for details.

You can even charter **fishermen's canoes** right off the beaches for day trips to secluded coves and offshore islands. The boatmen will help you catch and cook your picnic. Rates are highly negotiable, but a general rule of thumb is Rs13 per kilometre (0.6 mile) of sailing distance to cover petrol plus Rs12 per hour of the boatmen's time.

For a look at back-country Goa, try catching a **local train** from Vasco. They depart virtually any hour of the day and run to the beaches at Velsao or Cansaulim, the pretty Latinate town of Margao, the mansions of Chandor or the Dudh Sagar waterfall. At major bus stands, ferry slips or train depots, you are likely to be met by a fleet of **scooter rickshaws** and **yellow-painted motorcycles** which will take you wherever you are headed in the vicinity for one or two rupees per kilometre. Agree on fares beforehand.

If you are interested in longer forays, after-dark junkets, or just quick, spontaneous jaunts to choice restaurants, you will need your own transport. **Bicycles**, available for hire at about Rs20 per day, can get you from village to village without marring your appreciation of the sounds and smells that make Goa so special. But cycling gets pretty sweaty around midday, and your range is limited.

To roam further afield, you can rent **motorcycles** and **scooters** ranging from 50cc putt-putts to 250cc Czech-designed Yezdis. Day rates start at around Rs70, with discounts negotiable for longer terms. A month's use of a Yezdi currently goes for under Rs1,000 during peak season in the hippy Mecca of Anjuna. You pay for your own petrol. Also for maintenance, so be sure to check the condition of your bike before renting. Bike shops specialize in rentals in the main towns, as well as the more touristy beachside villages.

Individuals, too, are often quite willing to rent their own personal bikes. This can well turn out to be the best bet for shorter terms. To find one, just ask around bars, petrol pumps and shops.

To avoid bureaucratic hassles, better arrive with an international driver's licence endorsed for motorcycles. Bigger bikes are recommended for experienced riders only. Goa's twisty roads are no place for learner cyclists. Nor for daredevils: you share right of way with shambling cows, scurrying chickens, snoozing dogs, lumbering lorries and creaking ox-carts.

No self-drive autos are available, so if your party is too large — or too nervous — for motorcycling, your only other independent transport option is to charter a **chauffeured tourist car**. Per-kilometre rates run to Rs2.25–2.50 (still cheaper than the Rs3 per kilometre charged by yellow-top taxis), and often a flat day rate can be worked out at about Rs250. Some of the drivers are personable and knowledgeable enough to double as tourist guides. Ask your hotel to introduce one.

Food and Drink in Goa

One advantage of a 'creole' cuisine like Goa's is that, no matter where you come from, it is bound to taste exotic. Freshly arrived Western tourists are struck by the Oriental pungencies of turmeric and cumin, not to mention some of the hottest chilli varieties anywhere. But if your visit to Goa comes at the end of a long stint in India, you will find the local flavours curiously 'Western' and a refreshing change from the increasingly homogenized *masala* that is becoming the standard restaurant fare all over the rest of the country.

Ingredients, especially seafood, tend to be fresher and less overcooked in Goa. Pork, a rarity elsewhere in India, is a staple of the Goan diet. Coconut milk and sometimes vinegar figure in the sauces to take some of the bite out of the curries and make for a richer, more complex flavour. Goan cooks are more liberal with spices like nutmeg, cloves and cinnamon. Along with rice, the local cuisine features leavened breads rather than the unleavened flatcakes common elsewhere in India. Steamed dumplings, called *sana'an* or *odo*, are also Goan favourites.

Subtler than most run-of-the mill Indian cuisine, Goan cooking also requires a surer hand in the kitchen. No wonder that Goan cooks are of export standard. Chefs figure prominently among the emigrants Goa has been sending for generations throughout the subcontinent and around the world. They predominate in the galleys of merchant ships and the kitchens of five-star hotels. They are adaptable to any cuisine, from Chinese to Continental to Mughlai. But, like other Goan expatriates, they are prey to gastronomic nostalgia.

Each year in the pre-monsoon months of May and June, when other visitors shun Goa, out-of-state Goans flock home expressly to gorge on local delicacies. It is too hot at that time of year to do much

CHRIST THE KING II

(Clockwise from top left) Harvesting rice; busy market; fishermen take in their nets; Shri Mangesh temple at Ponda, Goa; boats of Christian fishermen

more than alternately eat and snooze. But that is more than enough for the true *cognoscenti*. Early summer is when the shrimps, lobsters and fish are abundant, the cashews and coconuts are ready for brewing into fresh *feni* liquor, the mango season is at its peak. Kids are on holiday from school and the Church obliges with a concentration of feast days, providing ample occasion for banquets.

In the expansive mood of one of these feasts — or Mardi Gras, or Christmas, or even just a village wedding — you might be lucky enough to land an invitation to a Goan home. That is by far the best place to sample the state's classic cuisine. But even if nobody happens to take you home for dinner, you can still get a pretty good sense of the delicacy and ingenuity of Goan dishes just by visiting local tavernas.

For Goans, unlike most other Indians, are convivial drinkers. Every urban neighbourhood and backwater village keeps two or three bars well patronized. Some of them boast three-page menus just to help wash down the *feni*. Featured items might include:

sorpotel, a vinegary stew of pork and pig's liver. The deluxe version, called *cabidel*, also adds pig's blood.

chorizo, the local variant of sausage, usually served in a red sauce.

xacuti, a high-octane curry smoothed out with coconut milk, cloves and nutmeg.

vindaloo-style pork or fish, prepared in a piquant gravy.

oyster guisado, a tomato-based soup.

steamed prawns, often in a yogurt-and-mustard sauce. This preparation also works well for lobster.

cabidela de pato, dried duckling slowly simmered in an earthenware casserole. According to the classic recipe, the duck should be plied with vinegar before slaughter and later simmered in its own juices. Tamarind features in the spicing.

Other menu items may be less exotic-sounding but are equally appetizing. In season, you cannot go wrong with seafood. Beach-front lean-to restaurants have enough sense to serve it simply-steamed, fried, grilled or baked. Mercifully, such places have sprouted up just down the strand from several of the five-star hostelries, offering denizens of these golden ghettos a needed respite from mediocre and over-priced hotel food.

To wash down your meal, Goa produces a line of distinctly Iberian-flavoured wines under the Adega da Velha label. The whites taste like sherry and the reds like port. For drier palates, stick to Golconda white and Bosca cabernet, both widely available. Or else sample *feni*, a distilled 'white lightning' spirit somewhat like Chinese Maotai.

Cashew *feni* is better as an aperitif than as a drink with food. It has a heavy, oily taste that clashes with some dishes. Uracco, the start-of-the-season distillate of young cashews (available only in the pre-monsoon) is lighter and more suited for table use. Coconut *feni* is also cleaner-tasting and more versatile. Ginger *feni* goes brilliantly with seafood. Drink it ice cold. Caution: *feni* can pack a wicked morning-after wallop. So can toddy, the sweet-sour undistilled palm wine that is the base for coconut *feni*.

Wherever you dine in Goa, be sure to save room for dessert. Better restaurants and tearooms boast a variety of pastries and puddings, including the classic Portuguese flan. But the undisputed queen of Goan sweets is *bebinca*, a multi-layered concoction of flour, eggs, coconut milk, butter and sugar that *aficionados* find irresistible, although it is as heavy as an ingot. For lighter appetites, mangoes round off a meal perfectly. Three Goan mango varieties are prized throughout India: Alphonsos, Fernandinas and Malcoradas.

Beaches of Goa

Beaches are why most tourists come to Goa, yet it is more than sun and sand that makes for the special cachet of this tiny stretch of coast. True, the broad, golden, palm-fringed expanse of shoreline, uninterrupted for miles on end, is as enticing as any beach on earth.

But no more so, intrinsically, than nameless strands up and down India's scraggly coastline, let alone those of neighbouring countries from Pakistan to Sri Lanka to Indonesia. But in many of these places, the beaches are either remote and inaccessible or teeming with fishermen, pilgrims and touts. Goa avoids either extreme. Villages live in close proximity and benign indifference to the seashore, offering basic amenities and diversions, but otherwise leaving holiday-makers to their own devices. Or at least, that is how it has been for the 30-odd years that Goa has been on the tourist map. The 'creole' culture of the place has been sufficiently pliant, yet firmly enough rooted, to resist successive onslaughts of flower children, five-star jetsetters and busloads of newly affluent Indian families from neighbouring states.

Nowadays, however, the strain is beginning to show, especially at some of the more established beach resorts, whose reputation is finally catching up with them. Cops routinely riffle through knapsacks in the tourist huts of **Anjuna**, **Calangute** and **Colva**, searching for drugs. Burglaries are on the rise, as much attributable to long-staying foreign beach bums as to affluence-dazzled villagers. Prude squads periodically prowl the beaches, forcibly clothing nude swimmers in a headline-grabbing byplay to political rivalry for control of Panaji's new-fledged statehouse (Goa achieved full statehood only in 1987).

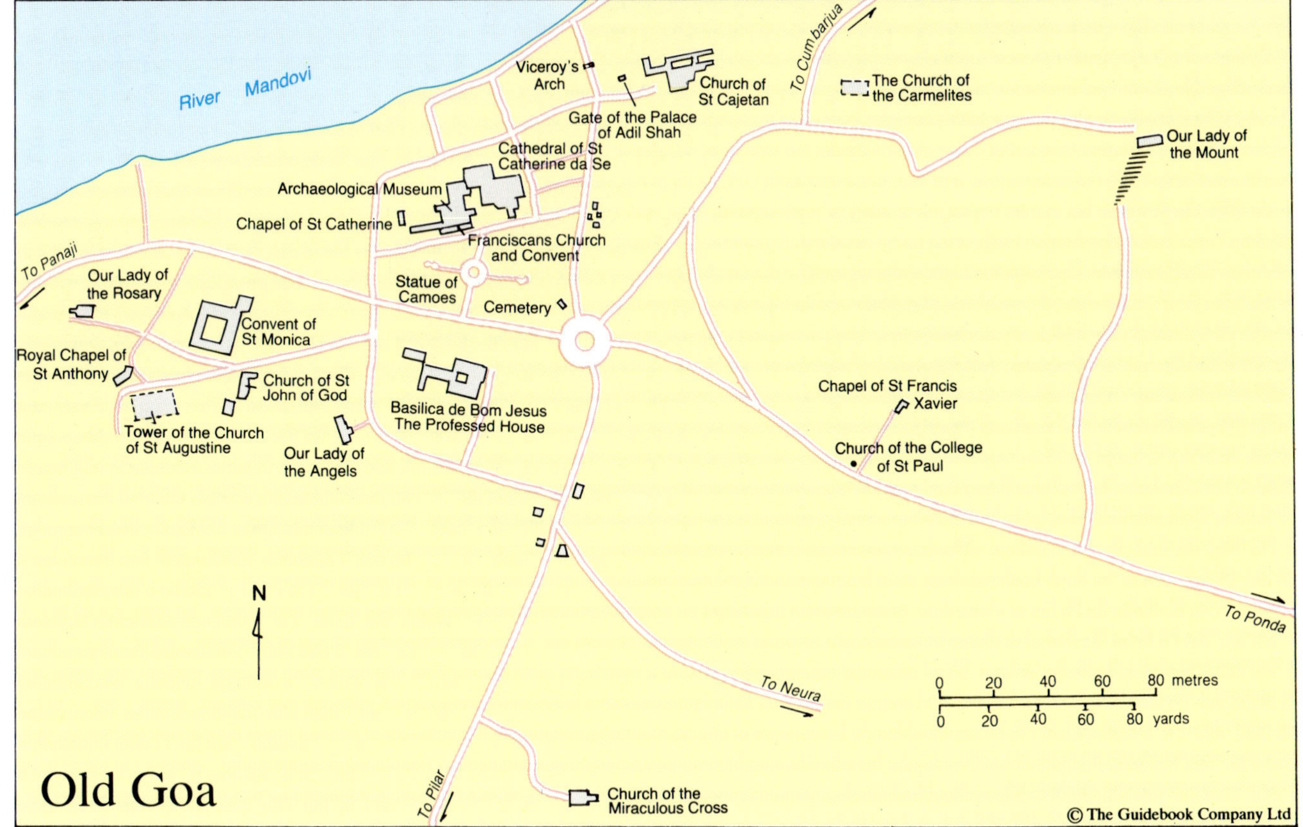
Old Goa
River Mandovi
Viceroy's Arch
Church of St Cajetan
To Cumbarjua
The Church of the Carmelites
Gate of the Palace of Adil Shah
Our Lady of the Mount
Cathedral of St Catherine da Se
Archaeological Museum
Chapel of St Catherine
Franciscans Church and Convent
To Panaji
Our Lady of the Rosary
Statue of Camoes
Cemetery
Convent of St Monica
Royal Chapel of St Anthony
Church of St John of God
Basilica de Bom Jesus The Professed House
Chapel of St Francis Xavier
Tower of the Church of St Augustine
Our Lady of the Angels
Church of the College of St Paul
N
To Ponda
To Neura
0 20 40 60 80 metres
0 20 40 60 80 yards
To Pilar
Church of the Miraculous Cross
© The Guidebook Company Ltd

Growing Commercialization

More government revenue and campaign funding is required under the new political order in Goa and the most readily realizable source is wholesale commercialization of the beaches. Indian and international hotel chains plan to nearly treble the state's five-star room count in the next few years. Palm groves are already giving way to high-rise hotels, which so distort the micro-economies of villages that it becomes impossible for locals to afford even fish at the height of the tourist season. So many five-star hostelries are now planned — 15 at the last count — that the tourist boom could turn into a bust through overbuilding.

Intermittent slumps in occupancy rates have forced even the present sextet of deluxe hotels — three in the Taj chain and one apiece by the Oberoi, the Welcomegroup and Holiday Inn — to resort to such expedients as offering deep discounts to Delhi-based diplomats and rouble-priced barebones vacation packages for Soviet groups. They also welcome non-residents to use their facilities for a fee.

That allows you to enjoy water sports and health clubs without paying five-star room rates or putting up with overpriced and joyless hotel restaurants. Small, tasteful hotels at **Dona Paula**, **Vasco**, **Benaulim**, **Candolim** and **Baga** (see pages 191–3) afford easy access to the facilities of their five-star neighbours. These are good bargains for families with children (charged at a fraction of the adult rate), especially if you have independent transportation.

Prize Beaches

Goa's prize beaches comprise virtually the entire coastline of two of the four *talukas* (counties) in the Catholic heartland: Bardez to the north of the Mandovi River, and Salsete, below the Zuari River. The strands stretch for mile after mile: in **Bardez** you can walk from the Taj group's **Fort Aguada Village** to the hippy redoubts of **Chapora** without ever losing sight of the surf — or the commercial glitz. Surf here tends to be rougher and the offshore shelf more precipitous than in Salsete.

South of the Zuari, the beach sands are packed hard enough for bicycling at low tide from **Velsao** to **Betul** — a total distance of nearly 30 kilometres (19 miles) — and the crisp lines of wave are ideal for body surfing. **Colva**, the first 'discovered' beach in the area, has already been over-developed, but neighbouring beaches remain unspoilt, at least for the time being. Deluxe hotels are planned here, and meanwhile the influx of young, budget travellers makes it hard to find accommodation even at once-deserted **Benaulim**.

Pluckier travellers can venture even further afield for a taste of what Goa beach life must have been like before the main tourist waves hit. Two hours by motorcycle or three hours by bus from Margao is **Chauri**, headquarters of Canacona *taluka*, which boasts a string of idyllic sandy coves along its rocky coastline.

The nearest of them, **Palolem**, an easy walk from Chauri, has a couple of seaside bars and accommodation for paying guests in the homes of local toddy tappers, but the main business of the town remains fishing and *feni*-running. The smuggling boat, a dhow-like sailing craft, leaves every Wednesday night after an uncharacteristically frenetic bout of loading activity on the part of the locals. A floating colony of Western castaways lives *au naturel* on an island at the end of the beach. **Agonda**, just north of Palolem, has been selected as the site of another five-star hotel. For the present, though, it is a kilometre-long (half-mile) stretch of virgin, palm-fringed beach backed by a friendly village with a grand, white 300-year-old church.

Similarly stunning beaches run the entire ten-kilometre (six-mile) length of the coastline of **Pernem** *taluka* at the northern end of Goa. This is Hindu country, so it is best not to rile local sensibilities by skinny-dipping. Beach-front accommodation is almost non-existent, but there is nothing to stop you from sleeping under the stars (as long as you look after your belongings; even here there are still enough foreign visitors to make burglaries a consideration). Or you could stay at the clean and very economical resthouse run by the state tourism department in the romantic ruin of **Tiracol Fort**, linked to the Querim end of the beach by frequent ferries.

Sights in Goa

The first thing that strikes the eye about Goan architecture, at least in the more Europeanized parts of the state, is its monumentality. The most obvious examples are the massive church buildings now stranded on the empty grass plains or overgrown hillocks of Old Goa, like shipwrecks on some green seabed.

But even in the less deserted surroundings of the villages of Bardez and Salsete, the parish churches seem outsized compared with the pastel shop-fronts and colonnaded bungalows nearby. It is as though the masonry itself was planned with missionary intent — hectoring, aggressive sermons in stone.

Lest the point is lost on the passer-by, crosses and chapels dot the roadsides, hilltops, river banks, seashores — any naturally arresting landscape feature. No coincidence, this: proselytizing Christianity made a conscious policy of usurping the sites previously occupied by Hindu or Muslim shrines.

The whitewashed assertiveness of the Christian monuments'

exteriors, though, is belied by the contemplative serenity of the interiors. Some are richly ornamented, most are soothingly simple. Clerestory windows diffuse the glare of the tropical sun, alcove chapels invite private meditation, vaulted naves and gilt retables uplift the eye.

The best time to visit Old Goa's churches is in the very early morning or around dusk. Not only is it cooler, but the crowds of tourists and village pilgrims are much thinner. Start with the **Cathedral of St Catherine da Se**, conceived in the eclectic Manueline style and generously proportioned (86 × 56 metres or 94 × 61 yards).

Eighty years a-building, the three-naved cathedral was conceived as 'a grandiose temple, worthy of the wealth, power and fame of the Portuguese who dominate the seas', in the words of the viceroy who commissioned it in 1564. Its glory is its retable, richly carved in three tiers, the topmost of which details the life of the cathedral's patron saint. Fifteen chapels ring the perimeter of the main sanctuary, each distinctively appointed.

You can climb the cathedral's one remaining tower (the other belfry was destroyed by lightning in 1775). Be careful, though: the experience can be somewhat jangling if you happen to be there at one of the five times a day they ring the carillon. The biggest of the five bells is called 'Golden' (Sino de Ouro) for its mellifluous tone, celebrated in a famous Portuguese poem.

The tower affords the best overview of Old Goa. Directly across the meadow-sized main square is the **Basilica de Bom Jesus**, the Jesuit church that houses the remains of St Francis Xavier. The **Franciscan Church and Convent** sits back-to-back with the cathedral to the southwest. To the northeast you face the **Church of St Cajetan**. The spindly ruin of the **Augustine Church** crowns the first ridge to the south, and beyond it, on a gentle rise, is the **Church of the Miraculous Cross**.

This last church may be Old Goa's least impressive, architecturally, but it is one of the most romantic. When a cross was erected there in the 16th century, water sprang from the rock in which it was set. The cross grew in size and Christ is said to have appeared on it, bleeding from his wounds.

It became a rallying point for indigenous Catholic priests who chafed under the colour discrimination that still prevailed in the European-established monastic orders in 16th- to 18th-century Goa. In contrast to Old Goa's grand, aristocratically patronized ecclesiastic edifices, the Church of the Miraculous Cross was built with donations from plebeian Goans, including a shoemaker buried near its portal.

The breakaway priests formed their own order, the Oratory of St Philip Neri, which survived (despite many defections) right up until the

expulsion of all religious orders from Goa in 1834. The Miraculous Cross itself was then moved to its present location in the cathedral.

The purge of the monastic orders was the death knell for many of Goa's noblest churches. Of the Dominicans, who ran the Inquisition, no physical trace remains. The **Augustine Church**, once the finest in the colony, collapsed piecemeal from 1842 (when the dome gave way) to 1931 (when the façade collapsed). Its vine-festooned ruins speak more eloquently of Goa's lost glory than many a better-preserved building.

The Augustinians' nunnery, the **Convent of St Monica**, escaped a similar fate simply because the colonial governors — chivalrous Latins despite their reformist zeal — could not bring themselves to turn out a community of women. But no new recruits were allowed, so the order aged and dwindled. Today, the functioning part of the chapel has contracted down to a few benches ranged in front of the ornate, baroque pulpit, hard by another miraculous crucifix, which is reported to roll its eyes, bleed and mouth words from time to time. Half the barn-like nave has been abandoned to bats and nesting swallows.

Another mood-piece is the oldest standing church in Goa, **Our Lady of the Rosary**, which is reached by following the road that runs under the massive buttresses of St Monica's until you come to a bluff overlooking the Mandovi River. It was from here that Afonso de Albuquerque watched his forces recapture Goa in 1510. The church itself dates back to 1543 and its style is stark compared to that of the later, grander edifices in Old Goa.

Built of unadorned laterite, its barrel-vaulted portal is flanked by turret-like towers that prop a square façade. The ribbed vaulting inside harks back to Gothic architecture, but the ornamentation incorporates peculiarly Indian motifs like cashews and mangoes. A white marble tomb in classic Bijapur style commemorates the low-born Portuguese wife of the tenth viceroy, the first European woman ever to come to Goa.

Just as old as Our Lady of the Rosary is the façade of the **Franciscan Church**, as attested by its clean geometry surmounted by two bristling octagonal towers.The barrel-vaulted nave was built a hundred years later. In contrast to the crisp exterior, the interior is a riot of ornamentation. Every surface seems carved, fluted, tessellated, stencilled, gilded or painted.

Cherubs snooze on lintels or prop up cornices. Saints and evangelists beam from their niches. Even the floor and ceiling are geometrically ornamented. The retable seems to fairly burst out of the apse in its sculptural exuberance. Flanking the main altar, 16 oil paintings detail the life of St Francis. A wooden pulpit is encrusted with floral carvings. The whole is suffused with light from the long windows of the apse and the clerestory.

The **Franciscan Convent** has been turned into a rather poky museum. The ground floor is given over to pre-colonial and Portuguese bric-a-brac. The upper storey features portraits of viceroys and other worthies, plus an interesting section of photos and documents relating to Goa's repeated native insurrections and its final 'liberation' by Indian forces.

In contrast to the Iberian heaviness of the church of the Franciscans and other religious orders, **St Cajetan's** has a spare, classical elegance in keeping with the Italian auspices of the Theatine order that built it. From the outside it looks like a miniature version of St Peter's in the Vatican. Inside, its Greek-cross layout is dominated by a dome directly over a mysterious well.

One theory has it that the well was sunk to drain off the soggy ground under the four massive piers of the dome. But the alternative hypothesis — that the church was built on the site of a razed temple — is borne out by the sanctity that Hindu pilgrims still ascribe to the well water.

Not that Hindus necessarily balk at venerating totems of strictly Catholic provenance. For instance, they come by the busload over long distances just for a *darshan* (sanctifying glimpse) of the relic of St Francis Xavier at the **Basilica of Bom Jesus** (see page 113). They file reverently around the mausoleum, a gaudy, three-tiered affair made of Carrara alabaster, multi-coloured jasper, purple marble, silver and crystal.

The mausoleum is crawling with sculptured angels and saints and inset with bronze plaques depicting St Francis' missionary adventures. Scenes from the saint's life are also detailed in paintings on the chapel walls and 32 bas-reliefs on the casket itself. The miraculously preserved mummy (somewhat shrunken now, swaddled in rich vestments and bearing an emerald-encrusted golden staff) peers out of the glass lid of the casket.

The rest of the church, with its riotous gilt retable and its stolid red laterite façade, attests to the wealth and temporal power of the Jesuits in Old Goa. So does the massive facade of the **Church of the College of St Paul** out on the Ponda road, all that survives of the institution that once spearheaded the Christianization of all of Asia and Africa.

Behind the basilica is the **Professed House of the Jesuits**, whose tranquil atmosphere today belies the bitter infighting that surrounded its establishment. The Franciscans so assiduously opposed it that the site had to be consecrated surreptitiously with a midnight mass in 1585. Similar rivalries led the Franciscans to try to limit the height of the cathedral's towers (lest the sound of the carillon drown out the bells of St Francis). The Franciscans also wrangled with the Augustinians for the right to establish the first nunnery.

It is hard to imagine such bitter rivalries in the deserted, run-down precincts of Old Goa today, where each building stands free and unchallenged amidst green emptiness, like an architect's drawing. It must have made more sense in the crowded jumble and claustrophobic intrigue of the ancient walled city, with so much money and power at stake.

To catch a sense of the sway wielded by the religious orders at their peak, visit the erstwhile **Jesuit seminary** at **Rachol**. The first thing that strikes you is the sheer size of the place, with its enormous courtyards featuring defunct fountain systems and vanished grape arbours. The sense of space is magnified by the long reticulated cloisters and corridors.

Its scores of rooms are crammed full of antique furniture and darkling, mouldering canvases. Hidden lookout towers guard its approaches, affording plenty of advance warning to shut its massive portals against any threat. There is an escape tunnel in the basement, but where it leads is no longer known. Another seminary, founded by the Capuchins at Pilar, features a museum of pre-colonial artifacts excavated from the ancient Kadamba capital of Goa Velha nearby.

If proselytization was part of the point of Goan colonial edifices, no better testimonial to its success can be sought than the **Hindu temples** around **Ponda**. The religious refugees from the Catholic heartland may have staunchly maintained their faith, but architecturally they succumbed to the Portuguese sway.

So we find an odd hodgepodge of baroque balustrades, cornices, chandeliers and ormolu in the temple precincts of **Shri Mangesh, Shri Mahalsa** and **Shri Shantadurga** — all the more disconcerting considering how sacred and ancient are the gods enshrined here and how heroically preserved they were from the depredations of missionaries.

This sort of uncritical architectural borrowing has hardly abated to this day, as witness the glitzy villas built by nouveaux riche guest-workers returned from the oil-booming Gulf. Crude and out of context as they may seem, even these gaucheries may mellow with the patina of about a century or two.

That, anyway, seems to be the lesson of the stately villas that nestle under the grand old *kaju* (cashew) and mango trees or the *supadi* (areca) and coconut palms of Goa's villages. Back when these trees were young, so too must have been the titles of many of the grandees who built the mansions.

Caveat Lector

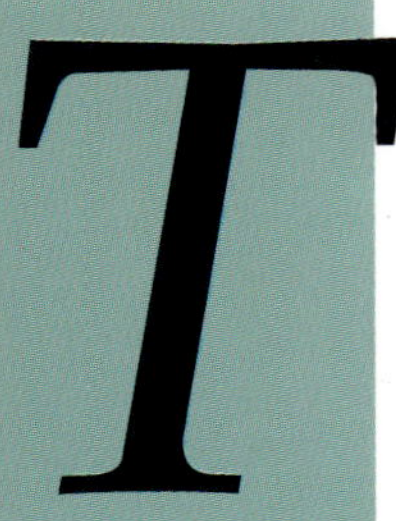

he government of Mysore commissioned me to write a travel book on Mysore. I was given a railway-pass for travelling within the state, a cash advance for expenses, and letters of introduction to various district officials asking them to give me 'all facilities'. Mysore State, extending up to Bombay in the north, Madras in the south-east, and Kerala in the south, offered inexhaustible material for a travel-writer, being rich in rivers, mountain ranges, forests, and wildlife, not to mention temples, monuments, and battle-scarred fortresses and ruins. By bus and train, I explored every nook and corner, listened attentively to the claims of the local enthusiast in any obscure mountain retreat or village lost in a bamboo jungle that here was to be found the earliest sculpture or civilization or the highest waterfall in the world, or that those footprints on a forest track were Rama's, or that the golden tint to that lily pond was imparted by Sita when she plunged in for a cool bath. In every place everyone found a token of a legendary hero or a mark left by the gods during a brief sojourn. Belur and Halebid temples, with their twelfth-century carvings, or the dungeons of Srirangapatnam, where in the seventeenth-century Tippu Sultan had kept his British prisoners, seemed modern in comparison. I climbed a peak of the Western Ghat to view the Arabian Sea coast, visible as a vibrant string of silver far off. And also I went down eight thousand feet underground to see a gold mine in Kolar, where the heat and pressure choked one's breath out.

I did somehow get through it all in the end, came back to Mysore with an accumulation of notes and data, and settled down to write my book. I was supposed to make good use of gazettes and blue-books, but found such reference work tedious and impossible, with the result that though my legendary tales and descriptions might beguile, the factful portions turned out to be unreliable. A friend in the Mysore Civil Service, who knew all parts of the state, marked in red the inaccuracies in my manuscript, and declared that the book should be kept away from any unwary traveller setting out to see the state. I believe I tried to save myself by appending 'about' or 'approximately' before every date or distance; with all that, I don't think my book has seriously misguided anyone.

R K Narayan, My Days: A Memoir

Noble rank, fiefdoms and administrative jobs (with the attendant opportunities for graft) were among the rewards accorded by the Portuguese to converts and collaborators. The Europeanized residences of these new-fledged dignitaries must have seemed the height of pretentiousness at the time.

Yet the families ripened into a genuine aristocracy over the generations. And the houses gradually filled up with the memorabilia of service in the far-flung Portuguese empire (which relied, far more than the British Raj, on natives of its earlier colonies to help administer its later ones).

Today, Goa's mansions are crammed with pottery from Macau, *ikat* from Timor, carvings and baskets from Mozambique and tapestries from Ormuz. Heavy, carved rosewood furniture, polished to a glistening sheen, chokes the grand ballrooms and parlours. Broad verandas and latticework false ceilings channel the breeze from room to room. Mature gardens spread their shade in the internal courtyards. Opalescent seashell windowpanes mute the tropical sunlight.

For all their opulence, though, most of these houses are not as daunting as their Western counterparts would be. All have a lived-in feel (indeed some are already a bit frayed) and many idiosyncratic touches. No two are alike: contrast the stained-glass mysteries of the Hindu **Deshprabhus' mansion** in **Pernem** with the Bohemian clutter of cartoonist **Mario Miranda's ancestral home** in **Lutolim**; or the austere river-front redoubt of the **Ynez de Castros** near **Ribandar** with the welcoming verandas of the **Menezes Braganca** in **Chandor**.

Few of these houses are set up as tourist attractions, prepared to receive raucous crowds. But if a villa seen from the road intrigues you, there is not much to lose by ringing at the gate and courteously expressing your interest. Chances are the flattered occupants may ask you in and regale you with family stories that bring the inert architecture and artifacts to life. A list of interesting Goa mansions, by no means comprehensive, is included at the back of the book.

Nor are the charms of Goan domestic architecture limited to aristocratic villas. Rows of gingerbread-style house-fronts line city squares in **Margao** and **Mapusa**, which also boast handsome covered markets. The red-tiled roofscapes of **Panjim**, when viewed from the peak district of **Altinhos** or the river approach by the ferry wharf, present a picture of Iberian quaintness that is somewhat belied by a close-up look at the rapidly redeveloping neighbourhoods.

Just around the riverbend from the Panaji waterfront, though, the old **Fontainhas** district seems little changed by the last two centuries. Pigs and chickens still meander through the jumble of streets. Lanes are so narrow between stucco house-fronts that the balconies almost meet overhead, yet the proud tenants find space for lush mini-gardens in the odd crannies of the defiantly non-rectangular street plan. Cobbled stairways mount bravely up Altinhos hill.

Tucked away in the tiny, dingy **Chapel of St Sebastian** in Fontainhas is the life-sized crucifix that used to hang in the Palace of the Inquisition in Old Goa. It is beautifully and realistically rendered. The head is unbowed, the eyes wide open, staring.

Festivals in Goa

The Hindu festivals in Goa are celebrated like anywhere else in the country. But the big events of the year are Easter, Christmas and New Year.

The three-day Carnival (February or March, three or four days preceding Lent), with its strong Latin flavour, is known to attract many visitors. Since 1987, though, when language stirs disrupted festivities, the state government has tried to play down the annual tradition. Now, the popular Carnival processions throughout Goa are less grand than before. But this still has not dampened the merriment.

Soon after the Carnival comes the Shigmo, which is the Goan version of Holi. The five-day festival concludes with the Rang Panchami, where people go about throwing coloured powder and water at each other and visiting friends.

Ajanta and Ellora

Masterpieces of Iconography

The cave temples of Ajanta and Ellora bear eloquent witness to two great upheavals in the religious life of the Deccan table and of peninsular India: the displacement in the seventh century BC of Hindu traditions by the 'reforming' religions of Buddhism and Jainism, and the resurgence of Hinduism, finally accomplished nearly a millennium and a half later in the eighth century AD (see page 142).

The caves at Ajanta were abandoned abruptly and mysteriously about a century before the Buddhist twilight in India. Ellora witnessed the swansong of Buddhist art, which shifted from a painterly to a sculptural emphasis. But the greatest masterpieces at Ellora are the Hindu caves. The energy of the friezes, the majesty of the architecture, the evolved iconography and teeming pantheon all bespeak the religious rejuvenation of the times.

Ellora's four Jain caves, physically removed from the rest, also stand at some emotional distance. They are the product of the conversion to Jainism of one of the Rashtrakutan kings late in the Ellora epoch, after the heat of the Hindu–Buddhist doctrinal debate had largely spent itself.

Perhaps it was a cooler conversion to a cooler religion than the earlier royal plunges into Hinduism. In any case, the resulting architecture is certainly less passionate, even somewhat mannered. None the less charming, though, for all that; technically the most refined in all the caves, with a proliferation of delicate detail.

Ellora, thanks mainly to the staggering Kailasha temple, could never really be overlooked and remained a pilgrimage site throughout its history. Its conspicuousness proved its undoing under the fanatical 17th-century Muslim emperor Aurangzeb, last of the great Mughals. A mob of his followers tore through the caves, systematically vandalizing every sculpture they could reach. (Aurangzeb's tomb is nearby, in case you want to pay your respects.)

The Ajanta caves, on the other hand, seem to have slipped from general memory for more than a millennium, until they were rediscovered in the early 19th century by a hunting party of British East India Company troops. Early efforts to record the Ajanta frescos seemed to be dogged by a mysterious curse. The Company deputed an artist who spent 27 years copying them, but his lifework went up in smoke while on display in London's Crystal Palace. Fire also destroyed the efforts of a Bombay team of copyists, whose paintings were the only important casualties of a fire in the British Museum. A Japanese

Reform and Resurgence

The history of the Deccan tableland has always had a Wild West frontier flavour that reflects its rugged terrain. The main line of Aryan advance into the subcontinent was far to the north, in the Gangetic plain. Harrapa colonies seemed to have flourished even earlier along the west coast. But only the backwash of these great migrations from the northwest reached the Deccan — a high, dry, inhospitable region, with plenty of hills but no major rivers, peopled by fierce tribes.

Even as late as the first millennium BC, when power was already consolidated in the Aryan heartland, the Deccan kingdoms remained linked to the great empires of the north only as loosely controlled fiefs. By that time, Vedic thought had already ossified into a sterile skeleton of ritual. Rigid caste delineations may have admirably suited the garrison mentality of a nomad people claiming new lands, but in a more settled age they act only to rankle the subject peoples and bolster a self-serving priesthood.

The time was ripe for a 'Reformation', and in the seventh century BC (roughly contemporaneous with Confucius and Lao-tzu in China, or Aristotle and the Hebrew prophets in the West), two great teachers emerged in India to sweep away the deadwood of Hindu doctrine: Gautama Siddhartha, the historical Buddha (or 'Enlightened One'), and Mahavira, the 24th and last Jain Thirtankar ('One Who has Crossed from the Material to the Spiritual Realm'). Both preached ascetic, reductionist doctrines that sought to strip away the veil of the material world's illusions and directly unite the devotee with the Absolute through meditation and austerities.

The new religions were originally preached by itinerant bands of mendicant monks, who came to rest in fixed monasteries (*viharas*, or rain shelters) only when monsoon rains curtailed their wanderings. They followed mostly the caravan routes, where they found receptive listeners and liberal alms-donors among the traders. Although increasingly rich from the burgeoning cross-Deccan traffic linking the Gangetic plain with the coasts, the merchants of the time were still relegated to a lowly caste status. So they welcomed the hierarchy-shattering messages of the Jains and Buddhists.

Buddhism found its 'Constantine' — its first royal patron — in the emperor Ashoka. From being dismissed as a subversive, rabble-rousing cult, it was suddenly propelled to the status of a state religion. Even after the decay of imperial power, it continued to enjoy the patronage of the increasingly independent Deccan kings. The caves at Ajanta and Ellora reflect the changing patterns of royal and mercantile patronage.

Drawing its main support on the one hand from kings, and on the other hand from the outcaste masses, Buddhism could no longer project itself as a 'small vehicle' (Hinayana) to carry a few elect ascetics to salvation. A new school of thought, the Mahayana ('great vehicle'),

fitted out Buddhism with a gallery of saints (bodhisattvas) with whom both the simplest and worldliest of devotees could identify.

Through prayer to these saints, devotion, philanthropy and ritual, the pious could escape rebirth. These innovations, which 'concretized' the religion, gave artists more to work with and greatly enriched the iconography. This shift is reflected in the Ajanta frescos. But the mystic and esoteric impulse reasserted itself late in the Buddhist epoch in the Vajrayana school, whose imagery predominates in the Buddhist caves of Ellora.

Vajrayana shared the Hindu tantric stress on cultivation of *shakti*, or subtle inner energies linked to elemental universal forces. Even these doctrinal borrowings, though, could not preserve Buddhism from the onslaught of the Hindu 'Counter-Reformation'. By the eighth century, royal and mercantile patronage had shifted away from Buddhism back to a reinvigorated Hinduism.

Buddhist group's rice-paper impressions of Ajanta's sculptures were destroyed in a Kyoto earthquake.

Restorers have not had much better luck than copyists at Ajanta. The Nizam of Hyderabad (in whose state Ajanta used to lie before India's independence) engaged a team of Italian experts to refurbish the frescos, but the varnish they used turned out to blacken with age.

The post-Independence Archaeological Survey of India (ASI) is struggling to salvage them, but the increasing tourist traffic — with its attendant erratic humidity levels, temperatures and vibrations inside the caves — has only made matters worse. At Ellora, the ASI is valiantly battling water damage to the carvings. Attempts to reconstruct some of the old stonework in reinforced concrete, however, have not always harmonized with the originals.

Getting To, From and Around Ajanta and Ellora

Getting There

Aurangabad is central to both Ajanta (104 kilometres or 65 miles away) and Ellora (28 kilometres or 17 miles), and features some lesser attractions of its own. It is the only place in the area offering international-standard accommodation, although quite comfortable, if simple, lodging can be found closer to each of the two sets of caves.

By Air

Indian Airlines has daily flights to Aurangabad from Bombay and a hopping service to and from Delhi via Udaipur, Jodhpur and Jaipur. Vayadoot also has a daily service to and from Bombay and Nanded, using the 19-seater Dornier aircraft, and a thrice-weekly service to and from Akola and Nagpur. Schedules frequently change (especially on Vayudoot) and delays are common.

By Rail

Aurangabad is on a metre-gauge line, which links it to Hyderabad and Manmad. Manmad is a junction on the Bombay to Agra line. If you are travelling by train, though, you need not pass through Aurangabad at all. The railhead for Ajanta is Jalgaon; for Ellora it is Chalisgaon. Both stations can be reached from Bombay by convenient overnight broad-gauge trains. Jalgon and Chalisgaon are nearly 24 hours from Delhi, if you are continuing up north.

From Jalgaon, Chalisgaon or Aurangabad, you can charter taxis to take you to the caves. State Transport Corporation (STC) buses are also frequent, interesting and cheap. They are far less crowded than the ones in Goa (let alone the municipal buses in Bombay), but getting a seat may still involve a certain amount of elbow technique. Privately run minibuses also ply these routes.

The main axes of the route network are Jalgaon–Ajanta–Aurangabad and Chalisgaon–Ellora–Aurangabad. But buses also run on the 76-kilometre (47-mile) route from Ajanta directly to Ellora, allowing you to cut out Aurangabad altogether. For short hops there are the ubiquitous scooter rickshaws and the occasional horse-drawn *tonga*. Hitch-hiking is also relatively easy and safe.

Getting Around

Cave walks can be surprisingly fatiguing, considering how short are the actual distances involved. But they combine the slow shuffle of a museum visit with the up-and-down trundling of a mountain hike and the neck-craning contortions of a spelunking expedition. All this in a climate that can get pretty warm at noon. Wear a hat, bring drinking water and maybe some energy-recharging snacks. Allow for rest stops or even midday siestas.

Guides will make themselves available to you at both cave sites. Choose one with care. A sensitive and well-informed guide with a good command of your language can really help bring the monument to life — well worth the Rs50–70 they charge for a full day's service. But a bad guide can be a burdensome hanger-on.

A guide is rather more useful at Ajanta than Ellora — the iconography is more varied and the frescos are full of telling details that are far from self-evident. Besides, your guide can mediate between you and the ASI factotums stationed at each cave to illuminate the interiors, either electrically or through the use of tea-tray-sized reflecting mirrors. These functionaries are keen to earn tips by explicating the caves. Their knowledge and language ability vary widely. The best of them are excellent on both counts. Bring a stack of one-, two- and five-rupee notes along to tip them according to their services.

Both the Ajanta and the Ellora cave complexes present a kind of theatre-in-stone, dramatizing historic and religious stories. For fullest impact, it helps to view them in the right sequence. The following itineraries are only suggestions. Vary them to suit your own schedule and interests.

Ajanta Walk

The cliff face in which the caves are carved lies in a horseshoe wrapped around a river bend. At one end of the arc, the Archaeological Survey of India (ASI) has set its kiosk where you buy your 50-paise entry ticket and your Rs5 light pass (without which the guards will not turn on the interior spotlights for you).

The sequence in which the caves occur (and are numbered) bears no relation to the chronology of their excavation. For a clearer sense of the evolution of art styles, religious ideas and iconography, you might prefer to start with the earliest caves, which are at the centre of the arc. Then work your way over to the left end of the horseshoe to sense the increasing architectural and sculptural sophistication of the caves as ornate Mahayana-influenced carving supplants the spare Hinayana style.

With this historic and plastic context established, you can proceed back along the entire arc focussing on details — especially the fresco paintings which, far more than sculpture or architecture, are the true glory of Ajanta.

For the venturesome, the most dramatic approach to the caves at the centre of the arc is along the river bed, which is how pilgrims originally came. The panorama of the rock face, the echo of the rushing water, the hum of cicadas and the arabesques traced by darting swallows all help to establish the majesty of the site. No wonder early animists deemed Ajanta the abode of a serpent king (whom the Buddhist artists incorporated into their own iconography as the cobra-shielded Nagaraja).

The approach along the river bed has the additional merit of being shadier and more level than the main path cut into the cliff-face. And it saves you the trouble of retracing your steps past the chronologically later caves at the right-hand end of the horseshoe. It involves two hassles, though: from the bus stop, you have to climb up the short hill to the ticket kiosk and back down again (send your guide if you have one), and then you have to ford the shallow river just beyond the rock vendors' stalls. There is always the alternative of the cliff-face path.

Across the river from the bus stop, a carefully groomed trail wanders amidst well-equipped playgrounds (handy if you have children along) for the first several hundred metres. It goes over a few dips and rises as the gorge narrows and the cave-studded cliff looms overhead. A sturdy bridge crosses over the neck of the gorge near a thundering (at least in the wet season) waterfall. Then some more manicured park before the path ascends in an easy grade up to a stairway that rises in between carved elephants just below cave 16.

Whether you approach via the river bed or the cliff-face path, begin with **cave 12**. This is a *vihara*, or monastic hall, dating to the Hinayana period (200 BC–AD 200). Its portico and interior paintings have weathered away, leaving just a spare, light-flooded, low-ceilinged box whose only ornamentation is the arched lintels over the niches and the doorways of the cells ranged around the three walls. This spareness of decor suggests the asceticism with which the monks pursued their meditations.

So does the clean architecture of **cave 10**, a *chaitya*, or worship hall, which is in the form of a long, barrel-vaulted colonnaded nave ending in a semi-circular apse almost entirely filled by a massive stupa. Early Buddhist artists borrowed the stupa shape from ancient funerary mounds that were used to entomb the ashes of saints. The stupa also represents an attempt to embody the abstract idea of nirvana, the state of blissful detachment that is the objective of meditation.

The stupa comprises a round dome (called *anda*, or egg) resting atop a cylindrical drum. The dome is in turn surmounted by a rectangular box that represents the reliquary. The whole is topped by a series of flat umbrella-style discs that suggest the sun shades of royalty as well as the peepul tree under which the Buddha attained enlightenment after 40 days' meditation.

The arboreal theme is emphasized by the avenue of trunk-like columns leading up to the stupa. The vault was originally crossed by purely ornamental wooden ribs suggesting tree branches (the sockets are still visible in the walls, and stone-cut ribbing still surmounts the side aisles). The pillars continue right around the stupa, underscoring the rhythm of the monks' circumambulations. To get a sense of the hypnotic power of the place, wait for a lull in the tourist traffic and then essay an 'Om' or two from the back of the apse.

Of the original Hinayana painting in this *chaitya*, only two fragments survive: a tableau of a royal processional en route to hear the Buddha's lecture (doubtless gratifying to the royal patron of the cave), and a scene from one of the Buddha's previous incarnations as an elephant (a theme that recurs in cave 17). The naturalism and detail of these paintings are impressive, but the colours are more muted than in later work and the perspective is flatter.

Mahayana amendments to the cave are to be seen in the figures of monks and bodhisattvas (enlightened beings who compassionately continue on earth to aid suffering humanity) on the pillars. If some of these look curiously occidental, it is no coincidence: they show the influence of Gandhara Buddhist artists from the upper Indus valley, whose ancestors came with the conquering armies of Alexander the Great.

Back outside, consider the massive tunnel-vault of cave 10 (so huge that, even choked with creepers, it was the only architectural feature of Ajanta that was visible, from a mountaintop far across the river, to the British hunting party that 'rediscovered' the caves in 1819). Instead of the wood-and-wire screen erected there nowadays by the ASI, this enormous arch was originally covered only with a screen of woven

bamboo and palm leaves to keep out birds and bats.

But, by the time they got around to building the neighbouring *chaitya* (**cave 9**), not long afterwards, the Buddhist cave architects were already going in for more ornate façades. The exterior arch, with its pointed stem at the top, recalls the shape of the peepul leaf. The concentric circular window is echoed in smaller circular patterns across the façade.

Under the overarching *chaitya* window (still left open for its leaf-and-thatch screen) are three smaller windows, with the screen reproduced in stone. Inside, the evolution of the stupa has already begun, with the enlargement of the reliquary, which here becomes an inverted pyramid.

By the time the next *chaitya* (**cave 19**) was built in the late fifth century, both artistic styles and religious thought had come a long way. This is the height of the renaissance of India's Gupta dynasty. The Mahayana epoch of Buddhism was well under way, with its heavenly hierarchies reflected in the teeming façade of the *chaitya*.

Standing bodhisattvas welcome the pilgrim with the open-handed gesture of conferring wealth. Seated Buddhas teach the law. Strapping guardian figures flank the *chaitya* window. The two standing Buddha figures alongside the colonnaded portico are rated the finest examples of Gupta sculpture. To the left of the door is a regal panel of the nagaraja with his consort and attendant. The whole façade is studded with cameos of animals, angels and lovers.

Inside, the 'trees' of the colonnade have sprouted carved foliage. In the capitals of the columns, seated Buddhas are serenaded by heavenly musicians. *Ganas* (gargoyle dwarfs) peer out from the fluted column shafts. Stone ribbing vaults the ceiling. The whole stupa has been encrusted with ornamentation and vertically elongated. The drum base and reliquary box have grown at the expense of the *anda* dome. The stone umbrellas are now supported by carved angels. A vase full of divine nectar has been added at the very top, touching the vaulted ceiling.

At the front of the stupa stands a life-sized figure of the Buddha, 'personalizing' the abstract message of nirvana and meditation, in the best Mahayana iconographic tradition.

That tradition had already reached its florescence by the late sixth century, when the last of the *chaityas* (**cave 26**) was excavated. The façade teems with Buddhas and bodhisattvas. The stupa inside is even more attenuated than the early Gupta version. Intricately detailed bodhisattvas ring the drum of the stupa and a large Buddha sits (European-style rather than cross-legged) at the front.

Almost at the end of the nave, a frieze shows how Siddhartha, on

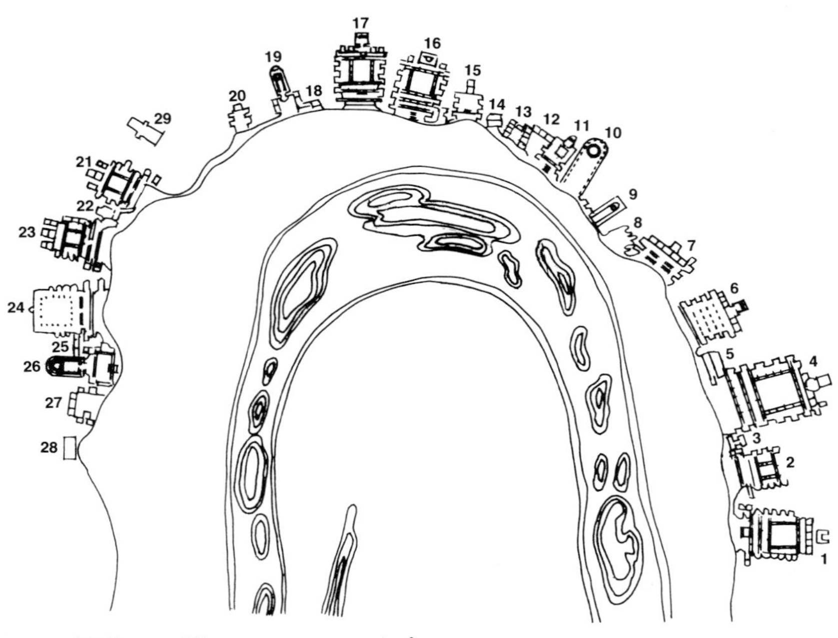

The Caves at Ajanta

the brink of enlightenment, was tempted by Mara (the Buddhist equivalent of Satan). Seated on an elephant at the upper left-hand corner of the frame, Mara directs his seven daughters — voluptuously detailed in the sculpture — to seduce the sage, while Kama, the Indian Cupid, stands by with his sugarcane bow at the ready. But the potential Buddha, under his peepul tree, is unmoved and the routed Mara is shown dejectedly retreating with his forces at the lower right-hand corner.

Amidst all the fussy baroque ornamentation of this last *chaitya*, the reclining figure of Buddha on his deathbed stands out as an island of calm. Its sheer size (seven metres or 24 feet long, by far the biggest figure in Ajanta) makes for large, uncluttered spaces. No drapery folds encumber the composition since the Buddha's robe, in keeping with the late Gupta convention, is denoted by just a wispy hem. But the overwhelming repose is best conveyed by the transfigured face (positioned so as to catch the diffused sunlight filtering in through the front door) and the languid hands.

On your way back around the arc of the cliff-face, stop in at **cave**

24, an incomplete *vihara*, for a glimpse of the excavation process. Only one column, in the front row on the right, has been finished. The rest are rough-hewn. The floor of the central courtyard is still just a jumble of uneven trenches crudely cut with a pick-axe. Yet one bracket capital is finely chiselled, the door is decorated with a frieze of flying figures and an outside chapel already enshrines a seated Buddha.

Incomplete caves like this show that the artisan-monks worked from the top down: verandas and ceilings were the first to be finished, with the central hall, sanctuaries and side cells chipped out later. The artisans of cave 24 were in the midst of this process when their work — and the entire Buddhist occupation of the Ajanta site — abruptly stopped for unknown reasons. Had it been completed, this would have been one of the largest caves at Ajanta.

Gross excavation and fine detailing seem to have gone on simultaneously. Other unfinished caves in the complex even boast finished murals. Walls were prepared for painting first by 'roughing' the surface with chisels and applying two layers — one coarse and one fine — of iron-rich earth mixed with cow dung and straw.

This laminate was topped with a thin layer of limewash on which the outlines were drawn. Then they filled in the colours. The technique used was a kind of tempera painting on a dry plaster ground with gum, instead of egg-white, as a binding medium. The paintings are not frescos in the technical sense, since the pigment was not applied to wet plaster. The term is used here loosely to denote a mural painted on a plaster ground.

The palette was limited to earth tones: red and yellow ochre, glauconite green, kaolin white and lamp black, all locally available pigments. The paintings were neither created nor originally viewed under the type of floodlighting provided nowadays for the tourist. Sunlight was channelled into the cave chambers by mirrors. During the painting, the central courtyards were flooded with water for extra reflectivity.

Even today, the attendants at many of the caves carry large mirrors as back-up illumination for the frequent power failures. Viewed this way, the effect of the murals is very different from under electric lighting. Colour contrasts translate into three-dimensionality, with the lighter portions almost floating on the darker backgrounds. In the flicker of the reflected light (due to passing clouds and movement of the hand-held mirrors) the painted figures seem almost to move. Imagine the effect on young novice monks or simple pilgrims listening to didactic sermons on the various saints, miracles and *jatakas* (tales of the bodhisattvas' prior incarnations) depicted on the cave walls.

Electric lighting, though, allows the modern visitor to take in at a

(Left) The Buddha achieves nirvana
(Top) Miracle of the thousand Buddhas, cave 2, Ajanta
(Above) Padmapani — masterpiece of Ajanta painting

glance the details and subtleties in the paintings that the original occupants of the caves might have noticed only through a lifetime of squinting at the walls. The murals awe you with the elegance of their composition, the feline grace of the figures, the expressiveness of the faces over the whole gamut of emotions.

They also contain a wealth of minute information about the material civilization of ancient India. There are scenes of palaces and villages and city bazaars, boudoirs and battlefields, sailing ships, deep forests — the list goes on and on, thanks mainly to the range of the *jataka* narratives. Nowhere is this topical eclecticism better displayed than in **cave 17**. Even before you go in, the veranda is alive with paintings.

To the left of the door, a prince and his consort share a last cup of wine before going to the city gate and distributing their worldly wealth to a collection of beggars. On the left-hand veranda wall is what remains of a gigantic and crowded Wheel of Life mandala. Right of the door, a crazed elephant rampages through a city bazaar, but then prostrates himself at the feet of the Buddha, who calms him with a compassionate touch.

Inside, various *jatakas* illustrate a bodhisattva's compassion, selflessness, spirit of service and other choice virtues in incarnations as an elephant, a monkey, a stag, a long-suffering monkey-bedevilled ox, a swan, a deer. The panel on the left-hand wall shows him incarnated as a prince who was so generous that his subjects had him exiled for bankrupting the kingdom. On the road to his banishment, he gives away first his horses, then his chariot, then his children and finally his wife to passing beggars.

Cannibalism provides the theme for two of the cave's *jatakas*. On the left rear wall, a bodhisattva weans away a prince from his pernicious habit of eating his subjects, an unfortunate side-effect of his parentage by a lioness. The prince's kinky conception and gruesome kitchen are all portrayed in detail. On the right-hand wall, the Buddha (born as a stag) helps a merchant-adventurer escape the clutches of man-eating ogresses disguised as beautiful maidens.

The front-most panel on the right wall depicts a king who rips out his eyes to give them to a blind Brahmin (actually a disguised god). The pilaster separating the ogresses from the eye-donor shows a dusky beauty admiring herself in her looking glass while her two maids-in-waiting look on. Cave attendants make a point of showing off how, when lit obliquely, the pearl ornaments of these figures seem to glow and stand out from the dark background.

At the back of the cave, the right-hand wall of the anteroom to the sanctuary features the Miracle of Saviti in which the Buddha multiplied himself a thousandfold in order to overwhelm a heretic opponent. On the opposite wall, he preaches to a large crowd including many foreigners. Mongolian and Persian facial features and dress are prominent in the crowd.

Not much is left of the paintings inside **cave 16**, but one surviving fragment makes this *vihara* worth a visit: the famous figure of the 'Dying Princess' on the left-hand wall, towards the front. Actually, she is not dying — merely fainting upon learning that her royal husband, Buddha's half-brother Nanda, has been persuaded to renounce the world (symbolized by the crown brought in by an attendant, left) and take up monastic life. Her swoon and the anxiety of her retinue are incisively portrayed.

Cave 2 presents the most impressive marriage of sculpture and painting at Ajanta. Flanking the main sanctuary at the rear are two smaller chapels. The left one contains two potbellied Kuberas (prosperity gods) whose sideswept, curly coiffure seems to have been the height of sixth-century fashion.

The busty lady seated in the right-hand chapel is Hariti, a fertility figure. She was an ogress who used to eat other people's children until the Buddha one day hid away her own favourite child. She retaliated with a furious attack (depicted in the frieze behind her in the upper left-hand corner), but was won over by the Buddha's doctrine of compassion (upper right-hand frieze). Her well-fed consort accompanies her, along with assorted attendants. On the pediment below is a schoolroom scene: the stick brandished by the master at the far right is evidently enough to cow the three front benchers into dutifully writing their lessons. But the next two boys are wrestling while the last five are goading a pair of rams to fight.

The paintings on the side walls of the Hariti chapel show elegant life-sized figures of female devotees bringing oblations. The craggy background landscape is especially worth noting. The corresponding figures in the Kubera chapel are not as well done, but the ceiling here features an exceptionally well-delineated mandala whose inner ring comprises 23 dancing geese.

Geese also figure in the *jataka* depicted on the front left wall of the cave, where the bodhisattva, incarnated as a goose king, is ensnared by a royal hunter and earns his freedom by preaching a religious discourse to a king and queen. Just beyond this on the same wall is the story of the Buddha's birth. His mother's dream of a white elephant (bottom left) is interpreted by a moustachioed astrologer. The pensive figure of the expectant mother is portrayed as voluptuously as a Hindu fertility goddess. The Buddha is effortlessly born from under her arm. The baby immediately takes seven steps (a lotus sprouting at each of his footfalls) and announces 'this is my last birth'.

Next to this is a panel of the miracle of the thousand Buddhas, a theme that is repeated on both walls of the chapel antechamber. Most of the right-hand wall is covered by a romantic story in which a general wins the hand of a *naga* (snake) princess (charmingly portrayed playing in a swing, centre). The *naga* queen, jealous of the favours showered upon her husband's wise counsellor (actually a bodhisattva incarnate) goads the general to challenge the king to a dice game (upper right). When the king loses, the general demands the wise minister as a prize. But all ends well when the minister beguiles both royal couples with his religious discourse.

Next to this *jataka*, at the front-most panel of the right-hand wall, is a scene whose narrative context has been lost, but whose expressive delineation counts as one of the masterpieces of Ajanta. A kneeling dancer begs for mercy at the feet of a sword-brandishing king. At the door of the cave, pause for a last look back at the ceiling painting, the best preserved of all the caves. No stories are depicted here: just a hypnotic swirl of floral and geometric motifs, angels, flying couples and comic dwarfs.

The same ornamental inventiveness marks the friezes carved on the veranda of **cave 1**. Dwarves, elephants and fighting bulls parade around the architrave. The left-hand end of this frieze shows a corpse, an invalid and a dotard — three sights that intruded upon the sheltered world of the princeling Gautama Siddhartha and propelled him to renounce the world. Inside, the same sculptural exuberance continues. The capital of one column even features four stag bodies sharing a single head — a type of *trompe l'oeil* the Ajanta artisans seemed particularly fond of, perhaps as a reminder of the illusory nature of all phenomena.

Such sculptural japes, though, pale before the dominant carving of the *vihara*: the giant seated Buddha in the central sanctuary, the finest such figure at Ajanta. Displaying the prescribed *lakshana* (signs) of enlightenment — the snail-curls, triple fold of the neck and elongated earlobes — he sits cross-legged, his hands in the *mudra* (gesture) of teaching.

The mood of the sculpted countenance changes according to the angle of illumination: sombre when lit from the left, blissful when lit from the right and serene when lit from directly below. The walls of the antechamber show again the Miracle of Savıtı, on the right, and Buddha fending off the hideous demon hordes of Mara, left.

The left-hand wall of the main *vihara* illustrates the stories of two kings who renounced the world: Buddha's half-brother Nanda, who parts most reluctantly from his heartbroken wife (see the 'Dying

Princess' of cave 16), and the contrasting story of Mahajanaka, who takes the monastic plunge despite the best efforts of his wife to entice him to stay. The panels towards the rear on the left wall show the king unmoved by the blandishments of dancing girls. After a last royal bath (upper right) he takes his leave on horseback, to the sorrow of his court maidens.

In between these two stories on the left wall is the *jataka* of the bodhisattva incarnated as a *naga* king, who tired of his sumptuous life and allowed himself to fall into the hands of a band of torturers. They drag him off by the nose until a passing commoner ransoms him. A similar story is related on the right rear wall, except this time the *naga* turns himself over to a snake-charmer until the *naga* queen begs the king of Benares to ransom him.

The two bodhisattva figures flanking the chapel on the rear wall of this cave are recognized as masterpieces of Ajanta painting. On the left is Padmapani, the lotus-bearer, a figure of Aryan finesse and almost feminine delicacy (in Chinese iconography he is transformed into Kuan Yin, goddess of compassion).

On the right is the dark, Dravidian figure of Vajrapani. His emblem is the masculine three-pronged totem of the thunderbolt, and his attribute is knowledge. By the time of the Ellora excavations, barely a hundred years after the last of the Ajanta caves, he had emerged as the central figure of the esoteric Vajrayana school, which then held sway in India and still dominates Himalayan Buddhism. Vajrapani here towers from floor to ceiling, his heavy jewellery standing out against his dark body, which in turn contrasts sharply with the exuberant green background.

Padmapani is no less towering a figure, but his body so lightly and delicately shaded as to provide a still area of calm against the joyous jumble of smaller surrounding figures — consorts, attendants, musicians, angels, monkeys, peacocks and lovers. The inward expression of his hooded almond eyes and the languid hand clasping the lotus enhance the serenity of the bodhisattva's figure.

The limbs and shoulders are rendered from different perspectives, but the subtle shading reconciles the contradictions. Still, the posture seems to shift from different vantage points — an illusion which enhances the phantasmagoric effect that is the hallmark of all Ajanta painting.

Ellora Walk

If you are rushed — which would be a great pity — devote your entire stay at Ellora to **cave 16**, the monumental **Kailasha**. More massive than the Parthenon and iconographically as rich as Chartres Cathedral, the freestanding solid mountain carved in the shape of a Dravidian temple cannot be viewed with even the most cursory appreciation in less than a day. At least scan the previous pages of this chapter to build up a rudimentary vocabulary of Hindu mythology. The Kailasha itself is covered on pages 170–5.

But, if you can afford a minimum of two days, start out by visiting some of the other 33 caves in the two-kilometre (1.2-mile) ridge of Chamadari Hill. Save the Kailasha for last, after a night's rest. That way, you can approach the masterpiece with the energy and concentration it deserves and see it in its historic, iconographic and artistic context.

If you mean to visit the other caves, bypass the parking lot in front of the Kailasha (where the bus stops). Instead, carry on to the right (as you face the temple), following the arc of the road to where it joins the arc of the ridge. This allows you to take in the whole sweep of the cave complex from a distance, without pre-empting the initial impact of your approach to individual caves.

The caves at this end of the ridge date from just about the time that Ajanta was mysteriously abandoned, in the sixth century. Buddhist excavations continued until about the mid-eighth century, by which time the Hindu resurgence was already in full swing. Hindu **caves** (numbers **13–29**) were built over a timespan that overlaps the late Buddhist excavations on the one hand and the earliest Jain caves (about AD 800) on the other hand. Jain **caves** (numbers **30–34**), clustered at the far end of the ridge about 500 metres (550 yards) from the rest of the excavations, continued to be built until nearly the end of the millennium.

Unlike Ajanta, the spatial, numerical and chronological sequence of the Ellora caves roughly correspond. So you can work your way down the ridge along the path that fronts the temples, skipping over the Kailasha and coming back to it later.

The ridge meets the road in an unassuming foot trail that runs along a small knoll. As you leave the highway, the engulfing calm of the meadow is palpable. Only the crickets and sparrows and wild flowers bid for your attention, and you sense that the Deccan plateau at your feet must roll on for miles with just the same gentle hum of activity.

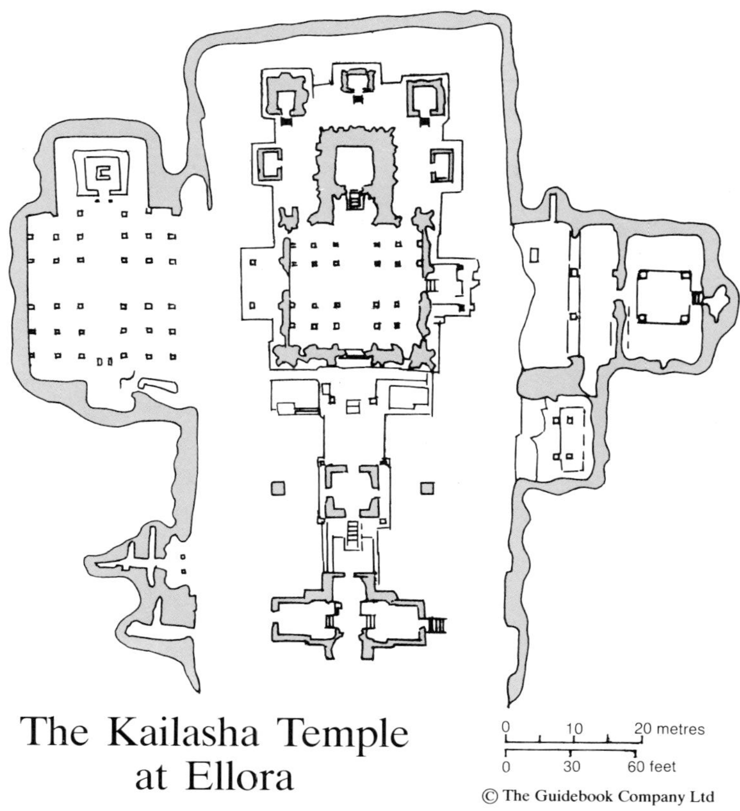

The Kailasha Temple at Ellora

Then, just beyond the knoll, the rock seam in which the caves are carved begins to open out — modestly, at first, barely the height of a man. But the calls of birds and insects take on the resonance of a stone sounding-board, and the arc of their flight stands out against the reddish rock backdrop. This subliminal interplay of fauna and rock will follow you throughout your Ellora visit. Meadow and mountain creatures, by their sound and movement, define the space here much more than at Ajanta.

For one thing, the Ellora caves are cut deeper and their facades are less enclosed. Then, too, they front directly onto the plain, rather than hanging halfway up a gorge. Ellora's site may be less dramatic than Ajanta's, but it is more 'alive'.

The procession of caves creeps up on you unassumingly. **Cave 1** is so chastely simple that archaeologists initially assumed it to be a storeroom, rather than a monastery (*vihara*). Senior monks may have practised the most advanced meditation here in the cells that radiate off the bare, uncolonnaded chamber.

Cave 2 seems to have been designed for more impressionable minds. Instead of side cells, the *vihara* features a colonnaded gallery running along the side with seated bodhisattva figures rhythmically arrayed in a row. Twelve massive, finely worked columns support the central courtyard. Gigantic, powerful bodhisattvas flank the main portals and the interior shrine. They are Maitreya, the Buddha to come, and an oddly muscle-bound Padmapani — a far cry from his languorous representation at Ajanta.

In the iconography of Ellora, the bodhisattvas' consorts are given extra prominence as embodiments of Shakti (female life force), much cultivated by the adepts of the esoteric Vajrayana school of Buddhism that prevailed here. Tara, consort of Padmapani, figures on the panel to the left of the main entrance to the shrine. The central Buddha figure is regal, seated on a lion throne, far more forceful than his introspective counterparts at Ajanta. **Caves 3** and **4** somewhat resemble cave 2, but they are more crudely executed — perhaps earlier essays.

Some of the simplicity of the first cave is recaptured in **cave 5**, but on a far grander scale. It is a *vihara*, open at the front, with cells along the periphery of its oblong colonnaded hall, which measures 36 by 17 metres (118 by 56 feet). Two raised ridges run along the centre of the floor. This is where the monks must have eaten and read their sutras. The image of them, drawn up in ordered ranks, suggests the discipline of an embattled army, as the Buddhists must have by now perceived themselves in the face of the Hindu resurgence.

At the end of the hall, like field commanders, preside the

bodhisattvas Padmapani and Vajrapani on either side of the main shrine. A deer head peers out from under Padmapani's left arm, a symbol of meditation alluding to the Buddha's first lecture after his enlightenment in the Deer Park at Sarnath in present-day Bihar. Inside the sanctum, the Buddha beams compassionately. But he is once again regally enthroned, seated 'European style', rather than cross-legged. His gauze-like robe is merely suggested by the finest of etching.

The cells in **cave 6** radiate off two oblong side halls rather than the central hall. The antechamber of the central shrine features an exceptionally graceful Tara panel on the left wall and a standing image of Mahamayuri, the Buddhist goddess of learning, on the right, with her peacock emblem. The iconographic resemblance to the Hindu goddess Saraswati is patent — a sign of the creeping syncretism that was to contribute to the extinction of Buddhism in India.

Padmapani, on the left side of the chapel door, has a deer skin slung over his shoulder and a small seated Buddha figure embedded in his coiffure. On the opposite panel, Vajrapani's thunderbolt (*vajra*) — a most powerful focus of Vajrayana worship — is shown not in the usual stylized three-pronged trident, but rather anthropomorphized in the little figure to the bodhisattva's left. In his crown is an image of the conventional trident.

The next three caves are relatively featureless, except for the freestanding sanctum of **cave 8**, which permits devotees to circumambulate the chapel. The shrine door in this cave is flanked by elegant, elongated figures.

The only *chaitya* (sanctuary, or worship hall) at Ellora is **cave 10**. Unlike the earlier *chaityas* at Ajanta, this one has a second-storey balcony above the front veranda. The grand, peepul-leaf-shaped window of the earlier *chaityas* has here been turned into a trefoil door flanked by heavenly nymphs and surmounted by flying couples symbolizing fertility. Bodhisattvas and their consorts occupy the niches on either side of the door. Above the right-hand niche is an amusing frieze of *ganas* (dwarfs).

Passing through the door, you are immediately struck by the rhythmic progression of stone-cut rafters across the barrel vault and the avenue of columns leading to the stupa at the end. This meticulous (and totally non-functional) imitation of wooden motifs has earned this *chaitya* the name of *sutar jhopadi*, the carpenters' workshop.

Perhaps this harking back to the wooden *chaityas* of the earliest Buddhist monasteries (and by extension to the forest groves in which the Buddha himself preached) denotes a longing for the days when the religion was simpler, purer and on the ascendant. The stupa itself, a clean and abstract form in the earliest *chaityas* (see page 147), is here

dominated by a life-sized Buddha figure, regally enthroned. By the time this cave was excavated (early eighth century), Buddhism in India was already reeling from the Hindu challenge.

The last two Buddhist **caves**, numbers **11** and **12**, represent more of a head-on response to this challenge. Three storeys tall, they are designed to instil awe rather than meditative contemplation. The first two storeys of each of these caves feature colonnaded arcades inset with monks' cells. But the third floors are large, open meeting halls studded with heavily carved figures of the bodhisattvas and their consorts.

The plan may have been grand, but the imagery — like the doctrine behind it — has already grown somewhat rigid and lifeless. By way of contrast, skip over caves 13 (a featureless box) and 14 (you can return presently) and go straight to the Hindu **cave 15**. This excavation is roughly contemporaneous with the multi-storeyed Buddhist *viharas* and laid out on a similar plan. It, too, consists of a relatively unadorned ground floor, with three rows of pillars and four cells, and a large, open hall full of sculpture on the upper storey. But how much richer is the iconography and how much more vibrant the sculptural style.

The side panels are deeply recessed in the walls, for a theatrical play of light and shade. The right-hand wall depicts the worldly manifestations of Vishnu, the preserver of the universe (hence the popular name for this cave, *dasavtara*, or ten manifestations). On the left and back walls are scenes celebrating Shiva, the regenerative destroyer, who is the main deity worshipped in Ellora's Hindu caves.

Many of these scenes will recur in subsequent caves, each time with slightly different emotional coloration. Starting with the left front panel and proceeding clockwise, the panels show:

• Shiva slaying the demon Andhakasura, who is seen in the upper right-hand corner impaled on a spear.

• Shiva as Lord of the Dance (Natraja), a powerful diagonal composition defined by the sweep of the left arm. Shiva outdid his consort, Parvati, in a dancing competition, since ladylike modesty prevented her from dancing with this much abandon.

• Shiva and Parvati playing dice on their Himalayan home, Kailasha ('Abode of Pleasure'), which is the very centre, or main axis, of the world. It is this entire mountain, no less, that the Kailasha temple (cave 16) sets out to symbolically recreate.

• Shiva marrying Parvati, who here appears very much the shy Hindu bride.

• The ten-headed demon Ravana, villain of the classic Hindu epic *Ramayana*, attempting to physically carry off Mount Kailash. Shiva, hardly even disturbed in his lovemaking with Parvati, steadies the mountain with his foot.

On the back wall, the two panels nearest the shrine are the most interesting. On the left side is Shiva straining the fall of the Holy Ganga's waters from heaven to earth through his matted locks (see page 97 on Elephanta). On the right is Shiva emerging from the primordial *lingam*. The *lingam*, a phallic shaft symbolizing creative potential, is Shiva's emblem. It is enshrined in the sanctum of this cave and all Shiva temples. The story of the original *lingam* is a neat piece of propaganda for the dominance of Shivaism over other Hindu cults.

Once, as the other two members of the Hindu trinity, Vishnu and Brahma, were squabbling about which of them was greater, a flaming shaft sprang up between them, stretching from the earth to the sky. Brahma turned himself into a swan and flew up to find the top, while Vishnu became a boar and burrowed into the ground in search of the bottom, but neither could get to the end of the column. As they returned to earth, defeated, Shiva stepped out of the flames and the other two gods knelt and acknowledged his supremacy (as they are shown here).

Yet despite the Shivaite auspices of Ellora, the left wall is devoted to Vishnu. He is shown here in his manifestations as:

- The god-king Krishna (here lifting a mountain).
- The primordial dreamer, reclining on the coils of an endless serpent adrift on the ocean of eternity. A lotus sprouted from his navel, from which emerged Brahma, who in turn created all things in the universe.
- Preserver of all things, here seen rescuing an elephant from the jaws of a crocodile.
- The giant Vamana, who spanned the universe in two strides and with his third step crushed a world-threatening demon.
- The Narasimha (man-lion) form he assumed to destroy a demon who had been promised immunity from being killed by man or beast.

This innately terrifying scene is here lightened by the dance-like flailing of the arms, by the rhythmic sway of the two bodies and, most of all, by the beatific expression on the face of the doomed demon. The balustrade next to the Narasimha panel makes a pleasant, breezy spot for a rest stop.

Then you can double back to **cave 14**, which is laid out on a plan similar to the Buddhist cave 8, with a freestanding chapel surrounded by a circumambulatory passage. Ornate pilasters along the two side walls separate deep-relief panels. On the left wall, starting from the front:

• Parvati in her fierce manifestation as Durga (the patron diety of Bengal) slaying the buffalo demon Mahisa.

• Lakshmi, goddess of wealth and contentment, perched on a floating lotus (note the watery creatures below). Pitcher-bearers and elephants sluice water over her in a ritual ablution (*abisheka*).

• Vishnu, incarnated as the boar, Varaha, rescues the earth goddess Prithvi (upper right) from a flood while the sea creatures venerate him with folded hands.

• Vishnu and his two wives.

Guarding the entrance of the shrine are the river goddesses Ganga and Yamuna. In the dimly lit recess behind the shrine is a panel of Shiva in his destructive aspect, mounted on a bull. This is followed by the figures of the Saptamatrika (seven mother goddesses), busty and heavy, each with a squirming child on her lap. The row culminates, as per convention, with an image of Lord Ganesh (Shiva's elephant-headed son, god of wisdom and auspicious beginnings) and the male and female death figures, Kala and Kali. This cadaverous pair is as scary as any mediaeval European Totentanz.

The right-hand wall of the main chapel features subjects that are already familiar from **cave 15**: Shiva impaling Andhakasura, Ravana shaking Kailasha, the Nataraja, Shiva and Parvati at their dice game, and Durga slaying Mahisa.

Double back now, bypassing the Kailasha, and follow the narrow road leading off the roundabout signposted for 'Caves 17–28'. In winter or the monsoon season, this is a delightful stroll, but it can be gruelling during the hot months. A scooter rickshaw can save you the hike. If you engage one, tell the driver to circle back along the road to cave 29 and wait for you. Although none of the intervening caves (with the possible exception of number 21) is all that interesting in itself, the cumulative effect is impressive. And the approach to the great cruciform **cave 29** is most impressive by trail, rather than road.

Cave 17 boasts one of the most complete and expressive Ganesh figures at Ellora. Ganesh is also featured in **cave 20**, along with Durga slaying Mahisa. **Cave 21** is one of the earliest Hindu excavations. A handsome Nandi bull (Shiva's vehicle) faces the shrine. The two river goddesses flank the door. Ganga (on the left) is particularly graceful and pert, almost coquettish.

The chapel inset into the left-hand wall depicts the marriage of Shiva and Parvati. The three panels (reading clockwise) show Brahma acting as a matchmaker between Shiva and Parvati's father, Himavan; the marriage ceremony (Brahma officiating as priest); and Shiva feigning *brahmacharya* (celibacy) while Parvati performs penance (their celebrated quarrels are an integral part of their amours).

Of the remaining Hindu caves in this row, only **cave 25** merits a stop for its standing figure of the sun god, Surya, in his chariot drawn by seven horses. Beyond the bare indentation of cave 28, the trail plunges down a stone cut stairway and then clings to the side of a massive, horseshoe-shaped cliff. Here and there unsophisticated idols peer out of box-like niches in the rock face. Swallows and lizards also nest here.

The trail passes directly under a great, arching waterfall that flows from the start of the monsoon through the end of winter. At the far end of the cliff-face, a steep flight of stairs ascends through a beetling tunnel. Then, abruptly, you emerge into the spacious **cave 29**. Sculpted lions guard the portals.

The cross-shaped floor plan has four transepts radiating off a colonnaded central hall. Three of them have portals, while the east transept ends in sheer, blank cliff-face (unlike the similarly laid-out Elephanta, see page 94, where the back wall houses the sculptural *pièce de résistance*). The west portal opens onto the plain, allowing the sunset glow to suffuse the cave. The south portal gives onto the cliff-face trail, and the north portal opens onto a rock-cut air shaft and a pool whose sacred waters pilgrims still come to bathe in.

In the centre of the cave is a freestanding sanctum with four doors, each flanked by enormous, stately guardians. The south transept features, again, the marriage of Shiva and Parvati, and the two of them playing dice. Capering dwarfs and a heavy, garlanded bull enliven the scene. In the north transept are tableaux of Shiva meditating and slaying Andhakasura. The main (western) portal is flanked by a Nataraja scene and Ravana shaking Kailasha.

Although massive and imposing, these carvings lack the finesse of later caves such as numbers 14, 15 and 16. Cave 29 dates from the mid-eighth century, when the Chalyuka dynasty was giving way to the Rashtrakuta kings. Cave 29 may be seen as a sort of rehearsal for such Rashtrakuta monuments as Elephanta and the Kailasha itself.

From the western portal, walk (or take your waiting rickshaw) down the curving hardtop road. At the first intersection, turn right to the Jain caves. It is a trek of about 800 metres (half a mile).

The best of the Jain caves date from the 11th century. What the carvings lack in force, they make up for in finesse. The attenuated figures, with their subtly expressive faces, bear as much stylistic resemblance to the European Gothic (with which they are nearly contemporaneous) as to the earlier Buddhist or Hindu carvings at Ellora. Cave 30, earlier than the other Jain caves and situated at some remove, is difficult of access and unfinished.

Cave 31, a small chapel alongside the door of the main Jain temple, introduces what is practically the sum total of Jain iconography. In the central niche, serenely meditative and marked with many of the same *lakshana* (signs of spirituality) as the Buddha figures, sits the Jain founder, Mahavira. He is 24th (and last) in the succession of *tirthankaras* (sages) recognized by the Jains.

His immediate predecessor, Parasnath, flanks him on one side, shielded by a cobra hood that denotes his mystic accomplishment. On the opposite side of the shrine is another *tirthankara*, Gomatesvara, who stood so rootedly on the spot of his meditation that trees and creepers grew upon his body. Aside from the foliage, he is wearing nothing else, for the Jain caves at Ellora were built by the Digambara ('sky clad') sect, which rejects clothing lest insects accidentally get snared in the folds of garments.

To mute the austerity of its doctrine for the benefit of common non-ascetics, the cave features a plump, sleek wealth god, Matanga (borrowed from the Hindu pantheon and also resembling the Kubera figures of Buddhist Ajanta). On the opposite wall sits the fertility goddess Siddhaika, looking very much like the Buddhist Tara or one of the Hindu Saptamatrikas.

This quintet is replicated again and again throughout **cave 32**, the main Jain excavation at Ellora. It figures in chapels that ring the ground floor of the courtyard. With its massive elephant and its monolithic tower (both sculptural 'quotations' from the Kailasha), the smallish courtyard seems overcrowded, all the more so due to the welter of ornamentation crammed into every available inch of wall space — *ganas*, exquisitely detailed foliage, models of stupa-like buildings, ranks of *tirthankaras* with their hands open in the *dana* (wealth-showering) *mudra* (ritual hand gestures). Amidst all the carving, outcroppings of virgin rock still erupt here and there for a striking contrast.

At the head of the stairway leading to the large, open hall on the upper storey, Matanga rides on his characteristic mount, an elephant. Siddhaika, on the opposite wall, sits on a lion and is surmounted by a fruit-bearing tree. Mahavira figures line the walls. He also reigns in the central chapel, along with his hieratic lion. Parsvanatha guards the chapel on the left. On the right stands Gomatesvara. His personal jungle, as rendered here, has acquired a population of snakes, scorpions, deer and other animals.

The columns, in the 'vase and flower' motif, are particularly well rendered. A giant lotus is carved on the ceiling and traces of the original paint are still visible. In the left rear corner of this hall, a rough-hewn door leads onto the upper storey of **cave 33**. The sculptures are equally fine and stand out better due to the uncluttered floor-plan (a simple, square hall with 12 pillars). **Cave 34** repeats the basic quintet of Jain iconography.

If you are staying the night (there is a comfortable, clean and only slightly overpriced hotel near the roundabout), you can treat yourself to a sunset walk that affords an overview of the Kailasha. Take the road from the Jain caves back to the roundabout facing cave 16. On either side of the massive excavation are stairways leading up the cliff-face. From the top you can walk all the way around the rock-cut temple. Indeed, this is the only vantage point from which you can see the whole of the Kailasha at once.

The **Kailasha** is laid out in the shape of a chariot, with the portico-cum-musicians' gallery in front representing the yoke. This is connected to the main shrine, or *mandapa*, by a bridge that supports the Nandi chapel — the 'shaft' of the chariot. The protruding transepts of the *mandapa* are the chariot wheels (at the great sun temple of Konarak, which is similar in layout, the transepts are actually embellished with giant wheels). The *mandapa* tower represents the driver.

At the same time, the Kailasha is meant to represent its mountain namesake, the abode of Shiva and Parvati. Originally the carving was all coated with painted plaster. Extensive traces of the original plaster remain in some places and the ASI is restoring it at other spots. This plaster was partly intended to figure the Himalayan snows on Mount

Kailash. At dusk (which is reliably spectacular at Ellora), the plaster catches the roseate glow of the setting sun.

Birds and animals, at least, seem to take the Kailasha in their stride as a natural mountain, rather than a man-made artifact. Bright green parrots, in tight flight formations, wheel about the *mandapa* tower. Striped squirrels scamper along the sculptured ridges. Pigeons and swallows nest in the walls. Mynah birds fill the space with echoing sound. Finches skirt about the base of the temple.

Even from the top of the cliff, it is far from obvious just where the base is. The first thing that strikes you is the *mandapa* tower, with its crowds of nymphs, *ganas*, leonine monsters (some in mid-copulation) and animals. But then you notice below this the relatively uncluttered space of the *mandapa* wall. The only carvings here are intermittent flying figures, which enhance the feeling of airiness. The tower-'mountain' seems to levitate.

Next, your eye settles upon the arcade behind the *mandapa* and the bridge through the Nandi sanctuary to the gallery. But even this broad horizontal expanse is not yet ground level. The whole temple rides on the backs of a row of massive elephants and other beasts moiling in the shadows far below. And under them is a plain pediment, taller than a man. And under that, all but lost in the dim sunset light, is the ground.

It is easier to envisage the excavation process from the cliff top than from down below. First, the central mountain had to be separated from the surrounding cliff. This they did by opening a fissure in the ground and driving in progressively thicker logs, which they then soaked with water so the wood would expand and crack the rock. Scooping away the debris, they repeated the process until they had a trench broad enough and deep enough to work with pickaxes.

Once they had a freestanding block, they began carving it from the top down. They must have had the complete temple planned from the start — the design does not seem to brook too much spontaneous improvisation — but it took an estimated 100 years to complete, from the mid-eighth to the mid-ninth centuries. Some 175,000 tonnes of rock are estimated to have been removed.

Note the magnificent hieratic lions on the rooftop, which must have been among the first things carved. They must be meant for the delectation of gods and rock-climbers; they cannot be viewed from anywhere within the actual temple precincts, as you shall see when you venture inside the following morning.

The doors of the Kailasha open at 6 am. If you go first thing in the morning, you can escape both the heat and the crowds. The portal itself is a kind of 'decompression' chamber to purge you of worldly anxieties and prepare you for the sacred abode of Kailasha. First you pass between the personifications of the sacred rivers, Ganga and Yamuna — a kind of symbolic ablution. On the left wall of the narrow entry passage sits the sage Vyasa, author of the sacred epic *Mahabharata*. Facing him on the opposite wall is Valmiki, who wrote the epic *Ramayana*. They represent the wisdom that can accrue to the devout.

Wealth, too, rewards piety, as symbolized by the fat Matanga figures in the broad antechamber beyond. Then the corridor narrows again, leading you past Ganesh (left) and Durga (right). They figure, respectively, auspicious beginnings and the conquest of evil. Four stately, smiling door guardians preside over the inner portal.

The first scene that confronts you is the image of Lakshmi, seated on her lotus, being sluiced with water by her attendant elephants. Note the little birds, frogs and flowers nestled among the lotus pads beneath her. The backward-swinging bells of the elephants offer a counterpoise to the upraised trunks.

Elephants — but trunkless ones — dominate the forecourt on either side, freestanding and nearly life-sized (the trunks were hacked off by Muslim vandals). Next to these animals tower massive fluted and carved pillars. The left one was originally capped by a trident and the right by a pennant. Turn left to begin your clockwise circuit of the temple (the prescribed direction according to Hindu rite).

The panels on the front wall feature Durga slaying the bull-demon, Krishna lifting the mountain, the love god Kama with his sugarcane bow and Vishnu riding piggyback on the avian god Garuda. At the end of this row, in a chapel cut into the north wall, stand the three slender, swaying figures of the sacred rivers Ganga (centre), Yamuna (left) and Saraswati.

The Saraswati has now vanished, if indeed it was ever physically real (a subject of scholarly debate, since nobody can convincingly point out even its dessicated channel). It symbolizes wisdom, just as the Ganga denotes purity and the Yamuna, devotion. Their depiction here might also commemorate a military expedition by the patron Rashtrakuta kings to the northern plains through which the three rivers flow.

Cross over to the plinth beside the staircase leading up to the main shrine. The detailed frieze here depicts, almost comic-book style, episodes from the *Mahabharata*. The plinth on the opposite side features a similar treatment of the *Ramayana* (positioned to the south since most of the epic's action took place in Sri Lanka).

The bottom two rows show episodes from Lord Krishna's childhood. In the centre of the first row, Krishna sucks dry the breast of a poison wet nurse sent to destroy him by his evil uncle Kamsa. She dies, but the poison imbibed turns Krishna the characteristic blue colour that he retains all his life. Near this scene, the mischievous infant Krishna manages to drag free of a grain thresher to which he was tethered by his harassed foster-mother. He steals the cream she is churning. On the lower panel, he strangles a crow-ogress sent by his uncle to attack him in his cradle. He slays assorted other demons, culminating with Kamsa himself.

From the vantage point of this plinth, look up at the ascending majesty of the temple and its tower. Directly before you is a line of huge, fabulous composite creatures seemingly supporting the whole Kailasha on their backs. The carving becomes increasingly attenuated as your eye travels upwards, until you reach the tower itself, which from this perspective seems to be writhing with foreshortened figures. The 'levitation' effect is even more pronounced from down here than it is from the cliff top.

A stairway leads up to a fine upper-storey hall cut into the cave wall. The columns and the caryatid nymphs are delicately carved. So are some — not all — of the erotic panels in the balustrade ringing the central courtyard. The hall affords yet another perspective on the overall temple.

For a closer look at the monsters and elephants atop the plinth, step up into the arcaded side galleries to your left. The sculptures on the wall here are not particularly fine, but the cumulative effect of light and shade is striking. So are the eye-to-eye views of the straining beasts supporting the *mandapa*. Each elephant is skilfully differentiated. The ones around the transept are straining and fighting with each other and with jungle animals. Towards the rear of the temple, the pachyderms stand stolidly in a row, as though stabled, munching on naturalistically detailed foliage and sugarcane.

Most of the stories in the side-wall panel are already familiar. A few new ones, though: the first panel on the north wall shows Ravana hacking off his surplus heads as an offering to Shiva, who is so impressed by the sacrifice that he promises that the demon will never be killed by any of the gods. That is why the legalistic Vishnu has to incarnate himself as the perfect man, Rama, to destroy him.

In the eastern gallery, panel 8 shows a composite figure of Shiva and Vishnu, suggestive of the syncretism that allowed the Kailasha builders to devote the entire southern gallery to incarnations and exploits of Vishnu (except for the first panel, which shows the androgynous Shiva-Parvati, see Elephanta, page 97).

The southern gallery ends squarely in front of perhaps the finest sculpture in this excavation — the giant, deep-etched, flailing figure of Ravana shaking Mount Kailash. In his subterannean cavern, the demon's 20 whirligig arms strain in all directions.

Shiva coolly tamps the peak back into place and Parvati merely props herself on an elbow (although the maidservant rushing in to warn them seems rather more perturbed).

The three-storeyed monastic hall directly opposite this sculpture offers different perspectives on the masterpiece. From the mid-level, the strain of Ravana is even more pronounced due to the foreshortening and the deeper shadows. From the top level, he is all but overshadowed, and Shiva's steadying foot dominates the composition. These terraces also provide good overviews of the south face of the temple.

Opposite the *Ramayana* plinth (whose thronging battle scenes somehow seem even more epic than the *Mahabharata*'s), a staircase leads to a chapel in the cliff-face with freestanding Saptamatrika figures and their usual attendants. The Kala–Kali images, perched on slithering piles of corpses, are particularly ghoulish.

Now you are ready to broach the temple itself. The porch under the Nandi shrine features two gigantic Shiva figures that sum up the god's contrasting aspects: the ascetic and the destructive. On the eastern wall sits Shiva the yogi, in serene meditation. The force of the triangular composition is all directed upwards. By way of contrast, the opposite panel (showing Shiva slaying an elephant-henchman of his old enemy Andhakasura) is a virtual mandala of violent radial thrusts in all directions.

The stairways flanking this porch lead up to the main sanctuary. Stop to visit the Nandi and then enter through the canopied portico. The ceiling of this canopy still bears traces of fine frescos (in contrast to most of the painting at Ellora, which bears no comparison to the Ajanta work). In the centre of the ceiling is a carved lotus. Love scenes grace the doorposts and Shiva himself acts as guardian figure.

The 16-pillared assembly hall is the flat-roofed structure visible from the cliff top. Its ceiling features Shiva Nataraja. Raised though it may be, with transepts on the north and south, the hall is still one of the gloomiest cave-interiors at Ellora, designed to instill awe and focus thought. You feel the weight of the mountain overhead. Shiva–Parvati scenes feature on the antechamber walls: the dice game on the left (with the figures now headless) and embracing on the right. The veneration-object in the shrine itself also represents a stylized embrace of Shiva and Parvati. A phallic *lingam* stands in the middle of a vulvate *yoni*. Priests, who were the only ones allowed in the sanctum when the temple was still consecrated, would pour libations over the *lingam*. The liquid would drain into the *yoni*, down a channel cut through the sanctum wall and into a catchment basin outside, where devotees could partake of the run-off as a sort of communion. This is still the practice in functioning Shiva temples.

The back of the sanctum is ringed with a terrace around which are ranged five freestanding chapels. Minutely detailed and designed in the same multi-tiered Dravidian style as the massive sanctum tower directly behind you, these shrines convey a feeling of miniaturization that can be pleasingly disorienting, especially when emerging from the gloom of the assembly hall and viewing the chapels against the looming background of cliff and sky. The libation basin is on the north wall of the sanctum. Although it is now dry, you can pause here for your private oblations before you leave through the purifying portals of the main gate to face the humdrum world.

Recommended Reading

History: General

Basham, A.L., *Cultural History of India* (Clarendon Press, Oxford, 1975)

Fischer, Louis, *The Life of Mahatma Gandhi* (Jonathan Cape, 1981)

Shearer, Alistair, *The Traveller's Key to Northern India* (Columbus Books, 1983)

Bombay

Chittar, S.D., *The Port of Bombay: A Brief History* (privately published, Bombay, 1973)

Cox, Edmund, *A Short History of the Bombay Presidency* (Thacker & Co., 1887)

David, M.D., *History of Bombay: 1661–1708* (University of Bombay, 1973)

Karkaria, R.P., *The Charm of Bombay* (D.B. Taraporevala, 1915)

Moraes, Dom, *Bombay* (Time Life Books, 1979)

Maclean, James Mackenzie, *A Guide to Bombay* (various editions between 1875 and 1902)

Proeschel, Diana and Merani, Saroj, *Flavours: A Selective Guide to the Eateries in Bombay* (The Perennia Press, Bombay, 1988)

Pusalker, A.D. and Dighe, V.G., *Bombay: Story of the Island City* (All-India Oriental Conference, 1949)

Tindall, Gillian, *City of Gold: The Biography of Bombay* (Temple Smith, London 1982)

Goa

da Costa, J.A.J., *A History of Goa* (Bombay, 1982)

Dias, Mariano, *Old Goa: Rome of the East* (St Francis Xavier's Training Centre for the Handicapped, 1984)

Doshi, Saryu, *Goa: Cultural Patterns* (Marg Publications, 1981)

Malgonkar, Manohar, *Inside Goa* (Directorate of Information & Broadcasting, Government of Goa, Daman and Diu, 1983)

Mascarenhas, Antonio, *Goa from Prehistoric Times* (Bombay 1987)

Menezes, Antonio de, *Goa: A Brief Historical Sketch* (AMA Travels, 1983)

Menezes, Antonio de, *Goa: Historical Notes* (Globo, 1978)

Nunes, Julia, *The Monuments in Old Goa* (Delhi, 1979)

Rajagopalan, S., *Old Goa* (Archaeological Survey of India, 1975, 1982)

Rayanna, P., *St Francis Xavier and His Shrine* (Bombay, 1982)

Ajanta, Ellora and Aurangabad

Barrett, Douglas, *A Guide to the Buddhist Caves of Aurangabad* (Bombay, 1957)

Dehejia, Vidya, *Early Buddhist Rock Temples* (Thames & Hudson, London, 1972)

Mitra, Debala, *Ajanta* (Archaeological Survey of India, 1983)

Pathy, T.V., *Ajanta, Ellora and Aurangabad Caves: An Appreciation* (Bombay, 1987)

Singh, Madanjeet, *Ajanta: Painting of the Sacred and the Secular* (Edita, Lausanne, 1965)

Verma, Umendra, *Illustrated Guide to Aurangabad, Daulatabad, Ellora and Ajanta* (Jayna Publishers)

Practical Information

Bombay

Hotels

What few good hotels there are in Bombay are relatively costly because of a hefty, government-levied tax on luxury. Clubs are good value but require some pre-planning.

Hotel services are liable to a seven per cent State Luxury Tax, a 20 per cent Expenditure Tax if the bill is paid in rupees and, occasionally, a ten per cent service charge. All foreign nationals are required to settle their hotel bills in foreign exchange (cash, travellers' cheques or credit cards). Major credit cards are accepted in India, American Express, Visa and Diners Club being the most universal.

Taj Mahal and Taj Mahal Intercontinental Apollo Bunder, Bombay 400 039. Tel. 2023366; tlx. 11 2442/6175 TAJB IN; fax. 2872711. 650 rooms including 42 suites. A good shopping arcade, health club, swimming pool, hairdresser, airline offices, florist and chemist. Single Rs1,950–2,150; double Rs2,150; suites Rs3,995–8,500.

The Intercontinental is the new wing of the hotel. The older Taj Mahal was built in 1903 by Jamshedji Nusserwanji Tata. Both have the same facilities, although the older Taj has more character, for which you pay a slightly higher charge (well worth it). The hotel faces the Gateway of India and the harbour while back rooms look out on downtown Bombay. So when making reservations be sure to specify your choice. Even if you are not staying at the hotel, make sure to look it up. The Bombay glitterati often show up for a fling. And the bookstore, Nalanda, is one of the best in Bombay.

Oberoi Towers and **The Oberoi** Nariman Point, Bombay 400 021. Tel. 2024343, 2025757; tlx. 11 4513/4154 OBBY IN; fax. 2043282, 2041505. 700 rooms including 48 suites. Oberoi Towers: single Rs1,950; double Rs2,150; suites Rs4,000–8,000. The Oberoi: single Rs2,200; double Rs2,400; suites Rs4,000–12,000. A large shopping arcade, good beauty salon, health club, swimming pool, business executive centre, airline offices and travel agencies. Very modern and the most professionally-run hotel in town. Located in the heart of Nariman Point, Bombay's new business centre, the Oberoi lies at the southern end of Marine Drive and on the west coast of the city. After seeing a stunning sunset here, you can hop into a horse-drawn carriage and ride along the Queen's Necklace — about a five-kilometre (three-mile) stretch of curved promenade — and have a *kulfi* at Chowpatty Beach.

Hotel President Cuffe Parade, Bombay 400 005. Tel. 4950808; tlx. 11 4135 PRES IN; fax. (022) 4951201. 319 rooms including 16 suites. Single Rs1,400; double Rs1,600; suites Rs2,500. Shopping arcade, hairdresser, health club, swimming pool, travel counter, bank and business service. The President belongs to the Taj Group of Hotels. Located at the southern end of town, reasonable rates, reliable service and some of the city's best restaurants.

Ambassador Hotel Veer Nariman Road, Churchgate, Bombay 400 020. Tel. 291131; tlx. 11 2918 AMBA IN. 127 rooms including 15 suites. Rates range from Rs1,100 to Rs1,400.

Fariyas Hotel Minoo Desai Road, Colaba, Bombay 400 005. Tel. 2042911; tlx. 11 3272. 80 rooms including two suites. Single Rs825; double Rs950; suites Rs1,600.

Hotel Natraj 135 Marine Drive, Bombay 400 020. Tel. 2044161; tlx. 11 2302. 82 rooms including nine suites. Single Rs925; double Rs1,050.

Ritz Hotel 5 Jamshedji Tata Road, Churchgate, Bombay 400 020. Tel. 220141, 220116; tlx. 11 2520. 72 rooms, single Rs860; double Rs985.

Grand Hotel 17 Sprott Road, Ballard Estate, Bombay 400 928

Sea Green Marine Drive, Bombay 400 020. Tel. 222294. The hotel at which Mahatma Gandhi's assassin stayed before he left for Delhi.

Salvation Army Mereweather Road, behind Taj Mahal Hotel, Bombay 400 039. Tel. 241824. Surprisingly well organized and clean.

Airport Hotels

The Leela Kempinski Bombay Sahar, Bombay 400 059. Tel. 6363636; tlx. 11 79236/79241 KEMP IN; fax. 6360606. A first-class hotel with 280 larger than average rooms and reasonable restaurants. Single Rs1,850, double Rs2,100, suites Rs3,000–11,000. 24-hour check in/out. Midway between international and domestic airports.

Centaur Hotel Juhu Tara Road, Bombay 400 054. Tel. 6126660, 6126678; tlx. 11 71171 CHTL IN. 288 rooms. Single Rs1,150; double Rs1,250. 24-hour check in/out. Half kilometre (third of a mile) from the domestic airport and four kilometres (2.5 miles) from the international terminals.

Welcomgroup Searock Sheraton Land's End, Bandra, Bombay 400 050. Tel. 6425454; tlx. 11 5460/6990 ROCK IN; fax. 6408046. 398 rooms. Single Rs1,500; double Rs.1,700; suites Rs3,500–5,000. Eight kilometres (five miles) from the domestic airport.

Holiday Inn Balraj Shahani Marg, Juhu Beach, Bombay 400 049. Tel. 620444; tlx. 11 71266/71432. 210 rooms. Single Rs1,200; double Rs1,400.

Hotel Airport Plaza 70-C, Nehru Road, Bombay 400 057. Tel. 6123390; tlx. 11 71365 PLZA IN. 79 rooms in this mid-range hotel whose biggest advantage is being close to the domestic airport. Single Rs550; double Rs700.

Clubs

Royal Bombay Yacht Club Apollo Bunder, Bombay 400 039. Tel. 2021014. 30 rooms. Single Rs350; double Rs605 — price includes three meals and tea. Temporary membership costs Rs250 for 28 days and includes use of the club's facilities. During the monsoons (June–September), however, boats are docked. Applications for reservations should be in writing and accompanied by recommedations from two club members and by an advance payment in Indian currency.

The Cricket Club of India D Vacha Road. Tel. 2040250, 220262. Has rooms for men only. Eight-day membership costs Rs200. Rooming costs for one week are Rs200 (single) and Rs400 (double).

Bombay Gymkhana plans to have residential rooms in the near future. The **Willingdon Club** has no room for guests.

Recommended Restaurants

South Indian

Kamat's Opposite Electric House, Colaba Causeway, Bombay 400 039. Tel. 2874734. A vegetarian restaurant, part of a South Canarese group. Open 8.30 am–10.30 pm.

Woodlands Near Opera House. An inexpensive, well-run vegetarian restaurant. Open 11 am–11 pm, closed Sundays. The Mittal Chambers branch recently burnt down.

North Indian

Copper Chimney Rampart Row, Fort, Bombay 400 023. Tel. 2041661. One of two restaurants of this name (the other is at Dr Annie Besant Road, Worli. Tel. 4924488) both serving good *tandoori* and other North Indian dishes. Open 12.30–3.30 pm, 7.30 pm–12 midnight.

Kabab Korner Natraj Hotel, 135, Marine Drive, Bombay 400 020. Tel. 2044161

Sheetal 648 Khar Pali Road, Bombay 400 052. Tel. 537746. Although this serves mostly North Indian food, the seafood is excellent. The expert can pick his own crab or lobster from the tank in the dining room. Open 11 am–12 midnight.

Khyber Kala Ghoda, Fort, Bombay 400 023. Tel. 273227, 273939, 273848. Recently renovated, this smart Punjabi restaurant not only serves excellent hot and spicy food but does so in extraordinary surroundings. Open 12.30 pm–4 pm, 7.30 pm–midnight.

Parsi

Bombay A-1 Grant Road Junction, 7 Proctor Road, Bombay 400 007. Tel. 381146, 399808. A cheerful restaurant opened in 1918. Also serves Mughlai and Chinese.

Britannia & Goa Wakefield House, Sprott Road, Ballard Estate, Bombay 400 038. Tel. 265264. Open 9 am–6 pm. A family restaurant run by Mr and Mrs Kohinoor, who prepare a separate fixed menu each day. Also serves Iranian (a speciality) and Mughlai.

Paradise Snack Bar Sindh Chambers, Colaba Causeway, Bombay 400 005. Tel. 232874. A family run-Iranian restaurant since 1956. Also serves Goan food. Closed on Mondays.

Piccolo Homi Mody Street, Bombay 400 023. Tel. 274537. An outlet for the excellent Ratan Tata Institute, which has a centralized kitchen. Open 9 am–6 pm with a new menu each day. Closed Sundays.

Goan

City Kitchen 301 Shahid Bhagat Singh Road, Fort, Bombay 400 001. Tel. 260002. One of the oldest and best-known Goan restaurants. Open 11 am–3 pm, 7–10 pm. Closed Sundays and public holidays.

New Martin Hotel 21 Glamour House, near Strand Cinema, Strand Road, Bombay 400 005. Popular local restaurant with plenty of hot, spicy seafood dishes (and some milder delights). Open 11 am–3 pm, 6–10.30 pm.

St Mary Hotel 120 St Mary Road, Mazgaon, Bombay 400 010. Tel. c/o 868475. A tiny (only six small tables) but well-established Goan eatery tucked away in a quiet corner of Mazgaon.

Saayba Hotel Bhatiya Building, opposite Bandra Masjid, S.V. Road, Bandra (W), Bombay 400 050. Mostly seafood. Open 11.30 am–3.30 pm, 7.30–11 pm; closed Mondays.

Maharashtrian/Mangalorean

Sindhudurg R.K. Vaidya Road, Dadar, Bombay 400 028. Tel. 4301610. Excellent *thalis* and other Malvani (Maharashtrian) dishes. Very popular with locals — always a good sign. Open 11.30 am–3.30 pm, 7–11.30 pm.

The Life of the Citizen

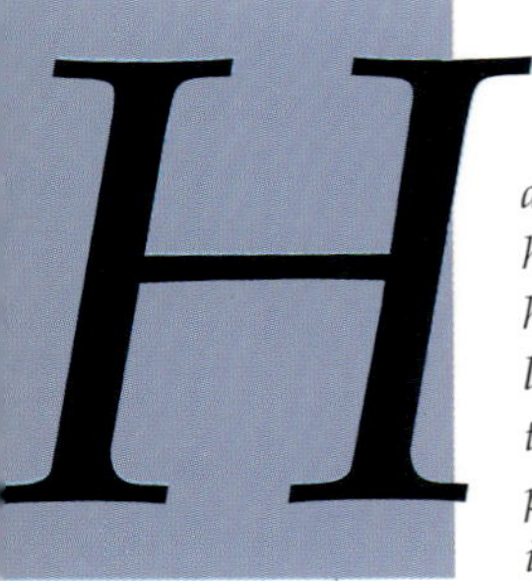

Having thus acquired learning a man, with the wealth that he may have gained by gift, conquest, purchase, deposit, or inheritance from his ancestors, should become a householder (Grihastha), and pass the life of a citizen. He should take a house in a city or large village, or in the vicinity of good men, or in a place which is the resort of many persons. This abode should be situated near some water, and divided into different compartments for different purposes. It should be surrounded by a garden, and also contain two rooms, an outer and an inner one. The inner room should be occupied by the females, while the outer room, balmy with rich perfumes, should contain a bed, soft, agreeable to the sight, covered with a clean white cloth, low in the middle part, having garlands and bunches of flowers upon it, and a canopy above it, and two pillows, one at the top, another at the bottom. There should be also a sort of couch, and at the head of this a sort of stool, on which should be placed the fragrant ointments for the night, such as flowers, pots containing collyrium and other fragrant substances, things used for perfuming the mouth, and the bark of the common citron tree. Near the couch, on the ground, there should be a pot for spitting, a box containing ornaments, and also a lute hanging from a peg made of the tooth of an elephant, a board for drawing, a pot containing perfume, some books, and some garlands of the yellow amaranth flowers. Not far from the couch, and on the ground, there should be a round seat, a toy cart, and a board for playing with dice; outside the outer room there should be cages of birds, and a separate place for spinning, carving and such-like diversions. In the garden there should be a whirling swing and a common swing, as well as a bower of creepers covered with flowers, in which a raised parterrre should be made for sitting.

Now, the householder, having got up in the morning and performed his necessary duties, should wash his teeth, apply a limited quantity of ointments and perfumes to his body, put some ornaments on his person and collyrium on his eyelids and below his eyes, color his lips with alacktaka, and look at himself in the glass. Having then eaten betel leaves, with other things that give fragrance to the mouth, he should perform his usual business. He should bathe daily, anoint his body with oil every other day, apply a lathering substance to his body every three days, get his head (including face) shaved every four days and the other parts of his body every five or ten days. All these things should be done without fail, and the sweat of the armpits should also be removed. Meals should be taken in the forenoon, in the afternoon, and again at night, according to Charayana. After breakfast, parrots and other birds should be taught to speak, and the fighting of cocks, quails, and rams should follow. A limited time should be devoted to diversions with Pithamardas, Vitas, and Vidushakas, and then the midday sleep should be taken. After this, the householder, having put on his clothes and ornaments, should, during the afternoon, converse with his friends. In the evening there should be singing, and after that the householder, along with his friends, should await in his room, previously decorated and perfumed, the arrival of the woman that may be attached to him, or he may send a female messenger for her or go to her himself. After her arrival at his house, he and his friends should welcome her and entertain her with a loving and agreeable conversation. Thus end the duties of the day.

The Kama Sutra, *translated by Sir Richard Burton*

Tambe Arogya Bhavan N.C. Kelkar Road, Dadar, Bombay 400 028. A Maharashtrian vegetarian restaurant popular since it opened in the 1940s. Open 8.30 am–2 pm (lunch from 11 am), 4–9 pm with dinner from 7 pm.

Gujarati

Chetana 34 K. Dubash Marg (Rampart Row), Kala Ghoda, Bombay 400 023. Tel. 244968. A mix of Gujarati and Rajasthani vegetarian dishes. Well located opposite the Jehangir Art Gallery. Open 12 noon–11 pm.

Thaili Tara Baug Estate, Charni Road, Bombay 400 004. Tel. 355934. Owned by a family from Kutch who reputedly often supplement the menu with their own dishes from their home on the first floor. Open 11.30 am–3 pm, 7–10 pm, closed Tuesdays.

Samrat Prem Court, Jamshedji Tata Road, Churchgate, Bombay 400 020. Tel. 220942, 222027, 220022. Serves a mix of Gujarati and Punjabi vegetarian food. Open 12 noon–10 pm.

Muslim

Bade Mian Sheekh Kabab Stall Tulloch Road, Colaba, Bombay 400 039. Located behind the Taj Mahal Hotel, this street stall serves some of the best food the city. You eat standing on the pavement, so not the place for a candle-lit dinner for two. Open 7 pm–midnight or whenever the last customer drives away.

Café Metro Near Metro Cinema, Dhobi Talao, Bombay 400 001

Gulshan-e-Tran Palton Road, Crawford Market, Bombay 400 001. Tel. 265183, 260748. Famous for its breakfast, this resturant continues to keep the ground floor an all-male preserve. Open 7 am–2 am the next day.

Do Tanki Near J J Hospital, near Police Post, Byculla

Delhi Darbar 197 Falkland Road, Bombay 400 004. Tel. 357977, 382589. Located at the heart of the red-light district on the corner of Grant Road, this huge restaurant runs different kitchens for the various aspects of Mughlai food. Open 8.30 am–3 am the next day.

Gulzar Hotel President, 90 Cuffe Parade, Bombay 400 005. Tel. 4950808. Good Hyderabadi and Pakistani food served in plush surroundings. Advisable to book in advance. Open 12.30–3.30 pm, 7.30–11.45 pm.

The Moghul Room Hotel Oberoi Towers, Nariman Point, Bombay 400 021. Tel. 2025757. Good buffet lunches, but the menu is worth exploring. Best to book in the evenings. Open 12.30–3 pm, 8 pm–12 midnight.

Kandahar The Oberoi, Nariman Point, Bombay 400 021. Tel. 2025757. Mostly meat dishes from the Northwest Frontier area of Pakistan. Open 12.30–3 pm, 8 pm–12 midnight.

Chinese

China Gardens Om Chambers, 123 August Kranti Marg, Kemp's Corner,

Bombay 400 026. Tel. 8280841, 8280842. Where the smart set often go to be seen as well as to enjoy a wide-ranging menu. Also serves Thai and Japanese dishes. Open 12.30–3 pm, 7.30–12 midnight.

Golden Dragon Taj Mahal Hotel, Bombay 400 039. Tel. 2023366. The original Szechwan resturant, with a new menu recently introduced. Open 12.30–3 pm, 7.30 pm–12 midnight.

Kamling Nagin Mahal, 82 Veer Nariman Road, Churchgate, Bombay 400 020. Tel. 2042618, 2045643. Bombay's oldest Cantonese restaurant, opened in 1938 by a group of homesick seamen. Open 12 noon–11.30 pm, closed over Chinese New Year.

Mandarin Dhanraj Mahal, Apollo Bunder, Bombay 400 039. Tel. 2023186, 2023832. Well-established restaurant near the Gateway. Open 12 noon–11 pm.

Nanking Pheroz Building, Apollo Pier Road, Bombay 400 039. Tel. 2020594. Still a popular and successful restaurant after almost 45 years. Famous for its fish ball soup and beef with watercress. Open 12.15–3 pm, 6.15–10.45 pm, closed for three days over Chinese New Year.

French

La Brasserie The Oberoi, Nariman Point, Bombay 400 021. Tel. 2025757. An expensive and smart coffee-shop that refuses to be known as such. Open 7 am–12 midnight.

Ménage à Trois Taj Mahal Hotel, Bombay 400 039. Tel. 2023366. The best French restaurant in the city, for which reservations must be made. Mostly nouvelle cuisine. Only open for lunches 12.30–3 pm.

La Rotisserie The Oberoi, Nariman Point, Bombay 400 021. Tel. 2025757. A smart and generally expensive restaurant but with some reasonably priced surprises; the 'businessman's lunch' is good value. Open 12.30–3 pm, 8 pm–12 midnight.

Apart from the above selection, the **coffee-shop restaurants** at the **Taj**, the **President** and **Oberoi hotels** all have interesting items on their menus and are open 24 hours. The President coffee-shop is part of a warm, friendly Italian restaurant: an unusual combination but one that works.

Useful Addresses

Tourist Services

Government of India Tourist Office 123 Maharshi Karve Road, Churchgate, Bombay 400 020. Tel. 293144

Maharashtra Tourism Development Corporation Express Towers, Madam Cama Road, Nariman Point, Bombay 400 020. Tel. 2024482, 2026713, 2027762, 2024627

Government of Goa Tourist Counter Bombay Central Station, Bombay 400 008. Tel. 396288

Central Railway Enquiries VT: tel. 2043535; Dadar: tel. 4133535

Western Railway Enquiries Churchgate (Headquarters): tel. 4933535

Airlines

Air Canada Hotel Oberoi Towers, Nariman Point, Bombay 400 021. Tel. 2027632

Air France Maker Chambers VI, Nariman Point. Tel. 2024818

Air India Air India Building, Nariman Point, Bombay 400 021. Tel. 2024142

Air Lanka Mittal Towers, Nariman Point, Bombay 400 021. Tel. 223299

Alitalia Dalamal House, 206 Nariman Point, Bombay 400 020. Tel. 222144

British Airways 202-B, Veer Nariman Road, Bombay 400 020. Tel. 220888

Cathay Pacific Taj Intercontinental. Tel. 2029561

Gulf Air Maker Chamber V, Nariman Point, Bombay 400 021. Tel. 2021626

Indian Airlines Air India Building, Nariman Point, Bombay 400 021. Tel. 2023031

Japan Airlines Raheja Centre, Nariman Point, Bombay 400 021. Tel. 2333136

KLM Royal Dutch Airlines 198 Khaitan Bhavan, J.N. Tata Road, Bombay 400 020. Tel. 221372

Kuwait Airways Veer Nariman Road, Churchgate, Bombay 400 020. Tel. 2045351

Lufthansa Express Towers, Nariman Point, Bombay 400 020. Tel. 2023430

Pakistan International Airways Oberoi Towers, Nariman Point, Bombay 400 021. Tel. 2021480

Pan Am Taj Mahal Hotel. Tel. 2029020

Qantas Airways Hotel Oberoi Towers, Nariman Point, Bombay 400 921. Tel. 2029288, 2029297, 2020410

Singapore Airlines Air India Building, Nariman Point, Bombay 400 021. Tel. 2023365

Swissair Maker Chambers VI, 220 Nariman Point, Bombay 400 021. Tel. 2870122

Thai Airways International 15 World Trade Centre, Cuffe Parade, Bombay 400 005. Tel. 215207

Banks

American Express 202 Dalamal Towers, 211 Nariman Point, Bombay 400 021. Tel. 222565

Bank of America Express Towers, Nariman Point, Bombay 400 021. Tel. 2023431

Bank of Tokyo Off Jeevan Prakash Mehta Road, Bombay 400 001. Tel. 2860564

Citibank 230 Sakhar Bhavan, Nariman Point, Bombay 400 021. Tel. 254836

Hongkong and Shanghai Banking Corporation 52–60 Mahatma Gandhi Road, Bombay 400 001. Tel. 274921

State Bank of India New Administrative Building, Madam Cama Road, Bombay 400 021. Tel. 2022426

Hospitals

Bombay Hospital New Marine Lines, Bombay 400 020. Tel. 2863234

Breach Candy Hospital 60-A Bhulabhai Desai Road, Bombay 400 026. Tel. 8223651

St George's Hospital Near GPO, Bombay 400 001. Tel. 4150246, 4150242, 4150344, 4151420

Ambulance Tel. 291255, 290582

Goa

Hotels

Goa has a large number of small family hotels and beach resorts whose reputations fluctuate with the season. A few, however, stand out above the rest.

The Aguada Resort Calangute. Tel. 87501-9; tlx. 0194-291 TAJ IN. A group of three hotels: the **Fort Aguada Beach Resort**, the **Aguada Hermitage** and the **Taj Holiday Village**, tel. 87514–7, run by the Taj Group of Hotels. If you choose to relax and enjoy all that Goa can offer for a holiday, this is the place you want. The Aguada Hermitage is one of India's most expensive hotels, but the Holiday Village is much more reasonable. The hotels link into each other and overlook Calangute Beach. They have their own bus link with the airport and Panaji, 17 kilometres (10.5 miles) away.

Sinquerim Bardez, Goa 403 515. Tel. 7501–9; tlx. 0194-291 TAJ IN

Cicade de Goa Vainguinim Beach, Dona Paula, Goa 403 004. Tel. 3301–8; tlx. 019-257 DONA IN. A Welcomgroup hotel, 27 kilometres (17 miles) from the airport and seven kilometres (four miles) from Panaji.

Oberoi Bogmalo Beach Bogmalo, Goa 403 806. Tel. 2191, 3311–5; tlx. 0191-297. Three kilometres (under two miles) from the airport.

Dona Paula Beach Resort Dona Paula, 403 004. Tel. 4255–6; tlx. 0194-221

Majorda Beach Resort Majorda, Goa 403 713. Tel. 20751–2; tlx. 0194-234

Prainha Cottages Reservations: Palmar Beach Resorts, 1st Floor, Glendela, Rua de Ormuz, Panaji. Tel. 4004. Newly renovated, has a private beach and reasonably good service. Good for families on low-budget holidays.

Mayfair Hotel Dr Dada Vaidya Road, Panaji. Tel. 5772–3. Simple and clean.

Hotel Mandovi D.B. Bandodkar Road, Panaji, Goa 403 001. Tel. 6270; tlx. 0194-226 SHOME IN. Centrally located.

भारताची
प्रख्यात
तीस छाप बीडी
30
REGD.
बेस्ट

Hotel Fidalgo 18th June Road, Panaji. Tel. 6291–9; tlx. 0194-213 REST IN

Hotel Riverside Baga Beach, Calangute. Beautiful location, 40 kilometres (25 miles) from the airport and very reasonable rates.

Recommended Restaurants

Hotel Mandovi Panaji. Tel. 4481

Longuinhos Bar & Restaurant Margao. Tel. 21038

St Anthony's Bar & Restaurant Calangute

Martin's Beach Corner Caranzalem. Tel. 4357

O'Coqueiro Alto de Porvorim, Bardez. Tel. 5671, 3628

Useful Addresses

Tourist Information Centres

Government of India Tourist Office Church Square, Panaji. Tel. 3412

Tourist Information Bureau, Government of Maharashtra Tourist Hostel, Panaji. Tel. 3572

Department of Tourism, Government of Goa Tourist Home, Pato, Panaji. Tel. 5583, 5715, 4757

There are **Tourist Information Counters** at Dabolim Airport (tel. 2644), in the Tourist Hostel, Margao (tel. 22513, 23766), the Tourist Hostel, Vasco da Gama (tel. 2673, 3119) and next to the Kadamba Bus Stand in Panaji (tel. 4132, 3459).

Transport

Air India Hotel Fidalgo, Panaji. Tel. 4081

Indian Airlines Dempo House, D. Bandodkar Marg, Panaji. Tel. 3826, 4067; tlx. 0194-219

Airport Tel. 2788, 3251, 3563

Railway Enquiries Panaji: tel. 5620; Margao: tel 22255, 2835; Vasco: tel. 2398

Shipping Agent (Bombay–Goa service) V.S. Dempo & Co Ltd, Campal, Panaji. Tel. 3842; tlx. 0194-217

Old Houses

House of Calasancio Souza at Aldona

House of Dr Gustavo Monteiro at Andolim

House of the late Dr Pinto at Anjuna, Bardez

House of Adv Sartorio Dias at Arpora, Bardez

House of Dr Alexei Pronenca, Calangute

House of Menezes Bragança at Chandor

Mansion of Dr Alvaro Loyola Furtado at Chinchinchim

House of Dr J Silva Pereira, Colva

House of Dr Maximo Menezes, Goa Valha

House of Dr Padrinho Gonsalves, Guirim

Mansion of Vicente Joao Figueiredo, Loutolim

House of Mario Miranda at Loutolim

House of Dr Armando Alvares at Margao

House of Fenoloa Rebello, Margao

House of Dr Eurico Silva, Margao

Mansion of Mr Rauraji Dashprabhu, Pernem, Villa

House of Mr Alvaro Jose Teofilo Pinto, Santa Cruz

Aurangabad, Ajanta and Ellora

Hotels

Aurangabad is not famous for its hotels, but there are two good properties which have all the necessary services, including swimming pools. The Taj Group will be opening a hotel in late 1990. Both hotels are on the road between the airport and the town and they usually provide a transfer from the airport.

The Ajanta Ambassador Hotel Chikalthana, Aurangabad 431 210. Tel. 82211, 82215; tlx. 0745-211

Welcomgroup Rama International R-3 Chikalthana, Aurangabad 431 210. Tel. 82455–7, 82241; tlx. 0745-212 RAMA IN

Aurangabad Ashok Dr Rajendra Prasad Marg, Aurangabad 431 001. Tel. 24520–9; tlx. 0745-229. This ITDC hotel is centrally located in the town next to the Indian Airlines office.

There is no luxury accommodation at Ellora, but there are some guest houses near the Ajanta Caves.

MTDC Holiday Resort Fardapur; five kilometres (three miles) from Ajanta.

MTDC Travellers Lodge Tel. 26; next to the entrance to the caves.

There is also an attractive turn-of-the-century **PWD Guest House** at Fardapur which can be booked through the Executive Engineer PWD, Padampura, Aurangabad (tel. 4874).

Index